REASSESSING LANGUA[GE]
AND LITERACY

Open University Press

English, Language, and Education series

General Editor: Anthony Adams
Lecturer in Education, University of Cambridge

SELECTED TITLES IN THE SERIES

The Problem with Poetry
Richard Andrews

Writing Development
Roslyn Arnold

Writing Policy in Action
Eve Bearne and Cath Farrow

Secondary Worlds
Michael Benton

Time for Drama
Roma Burgess and Pamela Gaudry

Thinking Through English
Paddy Creber

Development Response to Poetry
Patrick Dias and Michael Hayhoe

Developing English
Peter Dougill (ed.)

Reading Against Racism
Emrys Evans (ed.)

Children Talk About Books
Donald Fry

English Teaching and Media Education
Andrew Goodwyn

English at the Core
Peter Griffith

Literary Theory and English Teaching
Peter Griffith

Lesbian and Gay Issues in the English Classroom
Simon Harris

Reading and Response
Mike Hayhoe and Stephen Parker (eds)

Reassessing Language and Literacy
Mike Hayhoe and Stephen Parker (eds)

Assessing English
Brian Johnston

Lipservice: The Story of Talk in Schools
Pat Jones

Language and the English Curriculum
John Keen

Shakespeare in the Classroom
Susan Leach

Oracy Matters
Margaret MacLure, Terry Phillips and Andrew Wilkinson (eds)

Language Awareness for Teachers
Bill Mittins

Beginning Writing
John Nichols *et al.*

Teaching Literature for Examinations
Robert Protherough

Developing Response to Fiction
Robert Protherough

The Making of English Teachers
Robert Protherough and Judith Atkinson

Young People Reading
Charles Sarland

English Teaching from A–Z
Wayne Sawyer, Anthony Adams and Ken Watson

Reconstructing 'A' Level English
Patrick Scott

School Writing
Yanina Sheeran and Douglas Barnes

Reading Narrative as Literature
Andrew Stibbs

Collaboration and Writing
Morag Styles (ed.)

Reading Within and Beyond the Classroom
Dan Taverner

Reading for Real
Barrie Wade (ed.)

The Quality of Writing
Andrew Wilkinson

The Writing of Writing
Andrew Wilkinson (ed.)

Spoken English Illuminated
Andrew Wilkinson, Alan Davies and Deborah Berrill

REASSESSING LANGUAGE AND LITERACY

EDITED BY

**Mike Hayhoe and
Stephen Parker**

Open University Press
Buckingham • *Philadelphia*

Open University Press
Celtic Court
22 Ballmoor
Buckingham
MK18 1XW

and
1900 Frost Road, Suite 101
Bristol, PA 19007, USA

First Published 1992

A catalogue record of this book
is available from the British Library

Library of Congress Cataloging-in-Publication Data

Reassessing language and literacy / edited by Mike Hayhoe and Stephen
  Parker.
     p.   cm. — (English, language, and education series)
    Papers presented in the spring of 1991 at the Fourth International
Convention on Language and Learning held by the University of East
Anglia.
    Includes bibliographical references (p.   ) and index.
    ISBN 0–335–15798–X
    1. English language—Study and teaching—Congresses. 2. English
language—Study and teaching—Evaluation—Congresses.
3. Sociolinguistics—Congresses.
I. Hayhoe, Mike. II. Parker,
Stephen (Stephen James) III. Series.
LB1576.R425 1992
428′.007—dc20   92–5708
                                          CIP

Typeset by Graphicraft Typesetters Ltd., Hong Kong
Printed in Great Britain by St Edmundsbury Press Ltd
Bury St Edmunds, Suffolk

For Andrew Wilkinson, who planned the conference from which this book arose – and for Eileen Chapman, who did so much to ensure its success

Contents

List of contributors

Deanne Bogdan, Ontario Institute for Studies in Education, Toronto, Canada.

Brian Cox, Department of English Language and Literature, The University of Manchester, England.

Diana F. Davis, James Cook University of North Queensland, Australia.

John Dixon, Visiting Fellow, University of East Anglia, England.

Bernard T. Harrison, Division of Education, University of Sheffield, England.

Hilary Janks, University of the Witwatersrand, Johannesburg, South Africa.

Alison Littlefair, Consultant in Language in Education, Cambridge, England.

Peter Medway, Department of Linguistics, Carleton University, Ottawa, Canada.

Pamela J.K. Owen, St Martin's College of Higher Education, Lancaster, England.

James R. Squire, Executive Consultant and Editor, USA.

Leslie Stratta, LINC Coordinator, Midlands Consortium, England.

Preface

The papers assembled in this book were first presented in the spring of 1991 at the fourth International Convention on Language and Learning held by the University of East Anglia. The previous three conferences had focused on current thinking in specific areas: Writing, Oracy, Reading and Response. The 1991 event was designed by the originator of the series, Andrew Wilkinson, to celebrate a wider view of English studies in the year in which he was to retire. He was an ill man even as he started to plan; his courage and zeal were, therefore, all the more remarkable. Andrew Wilkinson died some two months before the convention took place.

This book brings together topics which emerged as being particularly significant in the immediate future. The first is the debate over the increasing intervention by the state and mercantilist ethics in education in general and, some would say, English in particular. Appeals to high and protected culture have less chance of success in this increasingly realistic, value-for-money world. Perhaps this is why the second theme arises, with several of these papers moving away from literature as a main focus of the English curriculum to transactional uses of language while other contributors debate how far these can be categorized and applied within the classroom. In this practical age, the third significant theme deals with the increasingly important issues of assessment and measurement. Arnoldian notions of promoting sensibility towards the numinous are fading at the dawning of a more practical world!

Yet there is optimism. The new realism can also drive and be driven by idealism, as the chapters about multi-cultural education show. In allowing his contributors an open space for his final convention, Andrew Wilkinson provided room for these themes to arise. Together, they demonstrate the importance of recognizing that English teaching exists in political contexts which seek to affect it increasingly strongly – and that we have the right and ability to affect those contexts in return.

Mike Hayhoe and Stephen Parker

General editor's introduction

The present volume is one in a series that we have published arising out of the biennial conference on English teaching that is held at the University of East Anglia. As the editors make clear in their own Preface and dedication, the conference was planned by Andrew Wilkinson who died before it took place. Andrew was a well-known contributor to this series and, as series editor, I would like to take the opportunity to join with the two editors in expressing my sadness at his departure. He leaves a serious gap both in the theory of English teaching and in the hearts of all who knew him.

However this book in itself represents a tribute to his work. Like its predecessors this conference had a strong international flavour and this book, which distils the work of some of the papers that were presented, contains distinguished contributions from across the English speaking world. The editors' own Preface indicates the range and scope covered by the volume and, in this Introduction, I would like to emphasize the political concerns to which they draw attention. As the book is being prepared for publication, a number of debates over the future of English teaching are taking place in England and Wales. There is a very real danger that many of the advances gained over the last fifteen years are to be imperilled by governmental interference. One of the several issues under discussion is the quantity of course work that will be permitted in public examinations at GCSE and A Level. This is a much more important issue than a mere argument over percentages. The kinds of student-centred approaches to English teaching that are taken for granted by many of the contributors to the present volume can only take place when students can choose their own contexts for writing. Many of the gains in understanding the writing process that are chronicled in this and other volumes in this series are threatened by what Hayhoe and Parker characterize as 'the new realism'. This 'realism' is not altogether new, however; rather it marks a potential return to outmoded methods and approaches, now discredited as an approach to English teaching throughout the English speaking world. It would be a tragedy if the country which did so much to pioneer the new approaches to English teaching was to be amongst the first to put these proven and successful approaches into reverse.

The first essay in the present collection is by Professor Brian Cox of the University of Manchester. His concern with the issue of English and National Identity is a very proper one. One of the important features of the Report of the Working Group on the English National Curriculum, led by Professor Cox, was its concern for extending the range of texts to be studied within English classrooms in England and Wales, to include literature from a wider range of cultures. This was a deliberate redrawing of 'the canon' of English teaching. Nothing could be more vital at a time when we are growing more conscious of the demands and opportunities of living in a pluralist society and moving towards a greater union with our neighbours in continental Europe.

Similarly, other countries represented by authors in this volume are undergoing momentous changes, not least South Africa, represented here by the chapter by Hilary Janks. This makes a clear case for the need to empower students through the development of what Janks calls 'Critical Language Awareness'. We may find an echo in the present government's attempt to stifle the work of the LINC (Language in the National Curriculum) programme of Janks's statement that 'Language is not an innocent medium . . . It is in and through language that the existing social order is contested'. In a similar way, writing from a Canadian perspective, Deanne Bogdan considers some of the problematical issues involved in widening the 'canon' of literary texts to be studied in schools.

The 1991 English conference at the University of East Anglia was deliberately conceived to be open-ended: the themes to be discussed were defined by the presenters rather than pre-determined by the conference title as on previous occasions. It is significant, therefore, that there should have emerged from so many contributors, far more than could be represented in this volume, a common concern with the issues of language and literacy within a political context. This has enabled the editors to provide a unified collection of papers out of what might otherwise have seemed very diverse material.

There is a need for the world-wide community of English teachers and scholars to resist the pressures towards a dull conformity, towards 'accepted' values and to continue to press for an English teaching that values all, irrespective of issues of race, gender and class. That kind of English teaching is celebrated in this volume as it was in the conference itself. It is to be hoped that in the pages that follow the reader will discern something of the international spirit of good-fellowship and goodwill that has characterized the four conferences with which Andrew Wilkinson was so centrally associated.

Anthony Adams

1

English studies and national identity

BRIAN COX

In his autobiography, William Whitelaw (1989) describes his shocked emotions when he was Home Secretary in 1980 during the time of the inner city riots in Liverpool, Bristol, Manchester and London. After visiting areas of smouldering fires, damaged cars and buses, and hysterical crowds, he at last returned for the weekend at his home in the countryside at Dorneywood in Buckinghamshire. He sat out of doors on a beautiful, hot summer evening, looking at the fields around Burnham Beeches: 'It was a perfect English scene,' he writes. 'Was it really in the same country as the riot towns and cities which I had visited during the week? Was it really in the same vicinity as parts of London a few miles away which at that moment were full of troubles? Surely, I thought, this peaceful countryside represents more accurately the character and mood of the vast majority of the British people.'

Such associations of the English countryside with the English national character are commonplace among Conservatives.

This pastoral myth is delightfully parodied in Kazuo Ishiguro's *The Remains of the Day*, which won the Booker Prize in 1989. Stevens, the butler, whose life has been dedicated to service of Lord Darlington, a leading advocate of appeasement in the 1930s, motors to Salisbury, stopping on the way to admire a typical English landscape. He tells us:

> the English landscape at its finest . . . possesses a quality that the landscapes of other nations, however more superficially dramatic, inevitably fail to possess. It is, I believe a quality that will mark out the England landscape to any objective observer as the most deeply satisfying in the world, and this quality is best summed up by the term 'greatness' . . . And yet what precisely is this 'greatness'? Just where, or in what, does it lie? I am quite aware it would take a far wiser head than mine to answer such a question, but if I were forced to hazard a guess, I would say that it is the very lack of obvious drama or spectacle that sets the beauty of our land apart. What is pertinent is the calmness of that beauty, its sense of restraint. It is as though the land knows of its own beauty, of its own greatness, and feels no need to shout it. In comparison, the sorts of

sights offered in such places as Africa and America, though undoubtedly very exciting, would, I am sure, strike the objective viewer as inferior on account of their unseemly demonstrativeness.

The English countryside, for Stevens, expresses a sense of restraint, a lack of drama or spectacle, without the unseemly demonstrativeness of Africa or America. It's not surprising that such images of tranquillity, restraint and passivity have such wide appeal for Conservatives, and that such underlying assumptions also become involved in their ideas about the National Curriculum and the canon of English literature.

The poem which encapsulates this mood most adequately is Philip Larkin's famous 'MCMXIV' (1964). In four carefully structured eight-line stanzas, with full rhymes and iambic rhythm, Larkin responds to a photograph of men queuing up to enlist in the 1914–18 war. He begins with details from the photograph – 'moustached, archaic faces', 'farthings and sovereigns' – and proceeds in the last stanza to a poignant lament for the loss of this age of innocence.

It is easy to pour scorn on the nostalgia expressed in this poem. Larkin longs for the supposed continuity of pre-1914 life – 'fields Shadowing Domesday lines', and the untrammelled existence of those golden days – 'the countryside not caring', 'the pubs/Wide open all day'. The nostalgia transforms the landscape into fantasy, as if in a child's illustrated fairy tale – 'The differently-dressed servants/With tiny rooms in huge houses'. In Hull, Larkin lived near Newland Park, where Edwardian middle-class houses provided an upper floor of servant accommodation with windows placed high up the wall so the staff could not see the family disporting themselves in the garden. In that pre-1914 period, working-class families were accustomed to low wages, long working hours in insanitary conditions, with death from tuberculosis a common phenomenon. However, the unique quality of this poem, I believe, is that Larkin implicitly acknowledges that his longing for continuity, tradition and order could never be fulfilled. The exquisite poise of the diction conveys a sense of vulnerability, a conservatism without hope.

This use of nostalgia and the pastoral has been brilliantly analysed in Paul Fussell's *The Great War and Modern Memory* (1975). In many writings about the war, such as the prose works of Siegfried Sassoon or David Jones's *In Parenthesis* (1937), the artist reaches out for traditional significance, attempts to re-attach traditional meanings to the unprecedented actualities of war. Trench warfare is meaningless and nauseating; language is used by many English writers to re-assert English cultural identity, often, as in Larkin's 'MCMXIV' by using images of pastoral continuity or by employing the connectives of grammar, rhyme and rhythm as a form of resistance to disorder. The nostalgic impulse works as an important agency in adjustment to crisis, a social emollient that reinforces national identity when confidence is weakened or threatened. Poems like Larkin's 'MCMXIV' bewail the loss of collective English identity, that continuity between past and present which derives a sense of sequence out of aleatory chaos. This English myth has dominated the imaginations of many readers of English literature, which for them stretches from the Wife of Bath to Falstaff to Pickwick to Jeeves. This concept of one nation is of great importance to Conservatives who still find solace in pre-industrial fantasies about our cultural heritage. They feel an instinctive trust in the works of English genius which for them ought to be enshrined in the English syllabus of the National Curriculum. Education is seen as a means of transmitting our cultural heritage; its ideological function is to reproduce culture and social order. A National Curriculum should impose from the top ranks of society a feeling of continuity, hierarchy and security which will help children to combat the post-modern condition of exile, alienation and disaffiliation.

This Conservative belief in the unity of the English tradition has inspired many apologia for English studies. In the Newbolt Report of 1921 (Board of Education, 1921), it is said (rather like Stevens in *The Remains of the Day*) that 'no Englishman competent to judge doubts that our literature ranks among the two or three greatest in the world: or that it is quite arguable that, if not perhaps the finest, it is the richest of all. Such a possession, once re-cognised as it is now, no university can afford to neglect.' These views are still common among some senior university academics. English literature is thought to preserve the unity of our cultural identity.

In *Cox on Cox* (Cox, 1991), in which I present my views of the National Curriculum in English, I describe how this emphasis on an English tradition has come under regular attack during the last twenty years or so; during their undergraduate training many young teachers of English will have discussed the assumptions that underlie such concern for our cultural herit-age. The desire for a unified national culture is seen as damagingly con-servative, often 'racist' and almost inevitably unsympathetic to the rights of women. This may surprise many people who read English literature for pleasure, and who would angrily reject any suggestion that they are conser-vative or racist. Is this not a piece of jargon? The argument rests not so much on the supposed responses of individual readers, but on the effects of institu-tionalizing an exclusive teaching of the great works of English literature. Only so much time is available in the classroom. Should we insist that children spend all their time with a literature whose main non-white representatives are Othello, Man Friday in *Robinson Crusoe* and the savages in Conrad's *Heart of Darkness*?

In England the desire for an 'English' tradition is said by some of its critics to hide a deep fear of our present multi-cultural society, a deter-mination to maintain our present class structure, the existing hierarchies of power. In the Working Group's recommendations (DES, 1988a) for the teaching of literature in the National Curriculum we tried to balance the arguments for national unity with the need for a curriculum which respected the present cultural diversity of our society (the same desire for unity and diversity underpins our recommendations on Standard English and dialects). On the one hand, we need national unity for the development of literacy, for common understanding of Standard English, for common values of tolerance, and equality of opportunity, justice and law, so we may live at peace with one another. At the same time we need to respect local differences, the need for diversity in our multicultural society, so that we may respect each other's dialects, each other's culture, each other's religion. A National Curriculum must not enforce one rigid, prescriptive role on teachers, but allow them freedom to develop their own initiatives. At the same time they need to give due attention to this kind of balance between different aims and purposes, in this case most specifically between the claims of an English tradition and of multicultural education.

We would all agree that children need stability and security for their upbringing. Should not schools provide an English Literature syllabus which gives their pupils that sense of continuity which Philip Larkin so desired, a sense of tradition and order, so that they can develop feelings of safety and self-confidence? Yet in our post-modern culture children will find, as adolescents, that they must come to terms with a society which offers no such stabilities and securities. Unless they choose a dogmatic religion, such as Moslem or Christian fundamentalism, they must take up the burdens of uncertainty under which most Westerners now live. If they proceed with literary studies they will learn to deconstruct the ideologies implied in conventional discourses and to contend with the cultural relativism implied in much post-modern thinking.

I believe very strongly that children need a sense of continuity and that we need to think very hard about where this is appropriate in our teaching of literature. A knowledge of English Literature before 1900 is valuable in its own right, and there is no reason why English children of all backgrounds should not be proud of the greatness of English writers such as Shakespeare and Dickens. Therefore, in our recommendations for the National Curriculum my Working Group emphasized the need for children up to the age of 16 to read pre-1900 literature in a range of genres, and in the final programmes of study which now have statutory force are listed Shakespeare, the Authorised Version of the Bible, Wordsworth, Jane Austen, Dickens and the Brontës. However, we were anxious to give teachers freedom to choose, not to impose on them a list of prescribed books.

Knowledge of English Literature is also of central importance in providing us with a common range of reference, and is of vital significance in developing linguistic skills in Standard English. The Kingman Report (DES, 1988b) says:

> Wide reading, and as great an experience as possible of the best imaginative literature, are essential to the full development of an ear for language, and to a full knowledge of the range of possible patterns of thought and feeling made accessible by the power and range of language. Matching book to the pupil is an

aspect of the English teacher's work which requires fine judgment and sensitivity to the needs of the child. It is good for children to respond to good contemporary works, written both for children and for adults. It is equally important for them to read and hear and speak the great literature of the past. Our modern language and our modern writing have grown out of the language and literature of the past. The rhythms of our daily speech and writing are haunted not only by the rhythms of our nursery rhymes, but also by the rhythms of Shakespeare, Blake, Edward Lear, Lewis Carroll, the Authorized Version of the Bible. We do not completely know what modern writing is unless we know what lies behind it. Hemingway's short sentences derive their power from their revolt against earlier more discursive styles. *The Diary of Adrian Mole* is a descendant of Dickens's urgent, knowingly innocent style. The apparently 'free' verse of D.H. Lawrence is imbued with the rhythms of the Book of Common Prayer.

These are some of the reasons why we recommended that all children should be given the opportunity to gain pleasure and critical awareness from the study of English Literature. At the same time we recommended that pupils should 'encounter and find pleasure in literary works written in English – particularly new works – from different parts of the world.' It is widely recognized that the most dynamic English today is often found outside England: from Saul Bellow, Alice Walker or Toni Morrison from the United States, Anita Desai from India, Nadine Gordimer from South Africa, V.S. Naipaul from Trinidad, Chinua Achebe from Nigeria, for example. In Britain, we confront daily the problem of a multiracial society; we have inner-city areas, such as London, Manchester or Bradford, where a large percentage of children may come from first generation immigrant parents. All pupils need to be aware of the richness of experience offered by writing in English from different countries, so that they may be introduced to the ideas and feelings of countries different from their own, and so we may help the cause of racial tolerance. In Britain today our multicultural problems must be taken into account by anyone establishing texts for a National Curriculum. Not only will children be introduced to a broader range of thought and feeling, but – through looking at literature from different points of view – pupils should also be in a position to gain a better understanding of the cultural heritage of English literature itself.

In an article in *The Independent Magazine* on 2 November 1990, Stephen Spender put forward ideas about a balanced curriculum very similar to those proposed by my Working Group. He confessed that study of the London and East Anglia Group Examination Board Curriculum, with its inclusion of multicultural texts, had persuaded him to change his previous opinions. Before 1945, Spender says, it was taken for granted that children of every kind of social background (particularly from the working class) should ideally speak and write an English which conformed with the standards of the best speech and writing of the educated upper classes. The purpose of teaching them the traditional classics was that they should meet these standards.

There really were no other standards; but in recent years we hear on the BBC new accents, new voices. Today our schools include thousands of children from various ethnic communities. The idea of 'correct' English as received pronunciation is no longer valid. The great tradition of Milton, Keats or Jane Austen, Spender says, is growing even further away from the present very fluid, Anglo-American language. Like many of the older generation, he finds this change unsettling. He writes: 'The idea of a future in which there is no single standard but a multiplicity of standards, each with its separate variety of correctness, is indeed terrifying'. However, he believes, as my Working Group did, that works by non-English modern writers must be included in the curriculum.

The study of literature, even in schools, must also take into account the revolution in literary theory which has taken place during the last twenty or so years. In the 1970s and 1980s, as faith among English teachers in our English national heritage or in Leavis's great tradition became less influential, there was a growing fascination with problems thrown up by the new methods of cultural analysis. In the Cox Report (DES, 1988a) we tried to balance the claims of our cultural heritage with those of cultural analysis. We listed two views of the subject both of which must figure in the teaching of English in the classroom: 'A "cultural heritage" view emphasises the responsibility of schools to lead children to appreciation of those works of literature that have been widely regarded as amongst the finest in the language.' Second: 'A "cultural analysis" view emphasises the role of English in helping children towards a critical understanding of the world and cultural environment in which they live. Children should know about the processes by which meanings are conveyed, and about the ways in which print and other media carry values.' This means that older children must be encouraged to discuss famous texts critically, must be aware of the reasons why the traditional English canon, from Chaucer to George Eliot, has been so much under attack in recent years. Sixth formers may enjoy reading David Lodge's *Nice Work* (1988), in which the fictional university lecturer, Robyn Penrose, reflects in her teaching and conversation the radical rethinking of literature teaching which is now commonplace in higher education. In polytechnics and universities cultural analysis is very often taught today in the context of post-modernism, and this could cause problems for the young graduates in English who go out to teach in secondary schools. What would Robyn Penrose's average student be telling his or her sixth formers about literature a few years after graduation?

Post-modernism, of course, covers a range of attitudes. I will try to deal with the central viewpoints which I often hear expressed by young lecturers, and which will certainly influence classroom practice in the future. In sorting out my own approach I have been particularly helped by David Harvey's *The Condition of Postmodernity* (1989). The post-modern critic expresses intense distrust of all universal or totalizing discourses, rejects all meta-narratives, all large-scale theoretical interpretations purportedly of universal application. No prescribed concept of identity must be imposed on the individual, and pupils and students must be offered a range of possibilities, must be encouraged to create their own meanings. The post-modernist prefers a plurality of styles, a lighter less rigid culture, diversity and provisionality, a heterogeneous range of styles which renounce any nostalgic urge to totalize and legitimate themselves. Post-modernism in the Western world reflects a vast change of sensibility, unsettling beliefs, codes, canons, procedures. The post-modern concept of the self is more protean and fluid than the so-called conventional repressed Western ego. Consciousness is forged of happenings, the immediate, performance, participation, the intense moment, the sensationalism of spectacle, rather than a sense of roots, continuity and tradition. One can see how this can translate itself in the classroom into the preference for dramatic spectacle, empathy in the study of historical personalities, passionate debate on contemporary issues, rather than careful study of evidence and the development of rational lucid analysis. Perhaps the main point is that in the classroom teachers of English in future are likely to resist the imposition of one prescribed identity for their pupils and are likely to want to help their pupils to discover appropriate styles of behaviour for themselves. The traditional model for the self, as exemplified by the public schools, is likely to seem a form of limitation, of repression.

So far I have tried just to describe the typical thinking of young teachers who distrust totalizing discourses in our post-modern age. This kind of thinking, of course, has been much criticized. Cultural relativism has been vigorously attacked by Allan Bloom (1987) in *The Closing of the American Mind*, who believes the result in the classroom is the smorgasbord of the American system, its inability to distinguish between the important and the unimportant in any other way than by the demands of the market. There is a sense of meaninglessness, the undermining of cultural foundations. At its worst the spirit of post-modernism leads to a state of anarchy, a lack of differentiation in concepts of the self.

How can the rejection of totalizing discourse avoid relativism or even anarchy? David Harvey draws useful distinctions between the negative and positive aspects of post-modernism. Post-modernism can be a liberating force, suggesting how in a multicultural society different concepts of reality may co-exist. Harvey writes: 'The idea that all groups have a right to speak for themselves, in their own voice, and have that voice accepted as authentic and legitimate is essential to the pluralistic stance of post-modernism.' In its concern for difference, for the difficulties of communication, for the complexities and nuances of interests, cultures, places and the like, post-modernism exercises a positive influence. It acknowledges the multiple forms of otherness as they emerge from differences in subjectivity, gender and sexuality, race and class, and spatial geographical locations and dislocations.

I would hope that children reared in this ambiance would be more tolerant, more understanding, less bigoted or rigid in their response to children from other cultural backgrounds. At its best, the rejection of totalizing discourses, of the nostalgia of William Whitelaw or Philip Larkin, creates new forms of imaginative awareness, new flexibilities and intimacies, and new possibilities for the self.

However, as Harvey explains, the post-modern emphasis on difference, its rejection of totalizing value systems, can be *harmful* to minorities: 'Worst of all, while it opens up a radical prospect by acknowledging the authenticity of other voices, postmodernist thinking immediately shuts off those other voices from access to more universal sources of power by ghettoizing them within an opaque otherness, the specificity of this or that language game.' This argument underlies my own passionate belief that all children must have access to spoken and written Standard English. Power in this country depends on the ability to use Standard English in speech and writing, in appropriate contexts, and on some degree of access to the English literary tradition, which is so deeply embedded in the language. If children are denied access to this discourse, they are marginalized, deprived of the resources needed to profit from and contribute to the wider culture, both national and international. The National Curriculum imposes Standard English and the English literary tradition on all children. Such collective action, such national planning, is essential if we are to help minorities, and this applies not only to education, but to many other areas: to transport, the environment, the Arts, where market values of supply and demand are insufficient. We may spurn grand narratives, total political solutions, total commitments, for example, to a market ethos, while accepting the possibility of limited action, of positive action to promote a sense of community and to develop in children the ideals of tolerance and respect for otherness, for local identities.

The teaching of English is of great importance in this quest for identity, both personal and national, because speaking, reading and writing provide roads to freedom, freedom from political control, freedom for the consciousness to pick and choose among competing value systems. This viewpoint is elaborated in relation to speech by Sylvia Adamson (in Ricks and Michaels, 1990). She explains how, for the structuralists of the 1970s, language was seen as a static, self-sustaining system, a tracery of prepared forms from which there is no escape. The language system determines all thought and expression; it is a prison-house whose inhabitants are deprived of free speech. Sylvia Adamson argues that in Saussure's distinction between *langue* and *parole*, whereas the language system is passively assimilated by the individual, speaking (*parole*) is an individual act: 'It is in speaking that the germ of all change is found. Every child is free in speech to create its own meanings, its own unique voice.' She discusses what might be deemed the paradox of the passive yet innovative speaker. She writes: 'The paradox appears not as a problem but as a solution. The solution depends on the existence of two kinds of meaning – on the one hand, meanings that are encoded in the vocabulary and grammar of the language and, on the other, meanings that arise contingently and by improvisation in particular contexts of speaking.'

So language as activity begins to impress itself upon language as a system, changing the code to accommodate the needs of its speakers.

I believe the same process takes place in our behaviour both as writers and readers, and that in these activities too we have the freedom to create our own meanings from the given language. The child in the classroom, just like a professional writer, needs to learn a craft, but very early on can begin to create his or her unique voice. In the teaching of reading we recognize the child's right to his or her own interpretations, and there has been much research in recent years into children's responses to their reading. Geoffrey Hartman sums up the freedom conferred by writing and reading in his *Criticism in the Wilderness* (1980):

> Each work of art, and each work of reading, is potentially a demonstration of freedom: of the capacity we have for making sense by a mode of expression that is our own, despite political, religious, or psychological interference. Because of the modern attitude that politics is fate, Malraux called art an 'anti-fate', and there is, at present, an adversary relation between civilised discourse and the political and technological drive for security – through thought control or the subordination of the arts (and even the universities) to specific practical ends.

This is why the reading of literature must remain at the centre of the curriculum.

In *An Appetite for Poetry* Kermode (1989) makes a crucial point about this freedom achieved through language. If this is to be achieved, then the words we read and the way we read must vary in *quality*. Kermode writes: 'historically the concept of literature is inextricably involved with the presumption of quality in both text and reader.' Post-structuralist devaluations of literature harm our respect for quality, for our freedom to evaluate and to assess and to praise greatness in writing.

To sum up, we need national unity, for the development of literacy, for common understanding of Standard English, for common values so we may live at peace with each other. We need to maintain our cultural heritage, which places great emphasis on individual freedom of expression. At the same time, we need to respect local differences, the need for diversity in our multi-cultural society, so that we may respect each other's dialects, each other's culture, each other's religion. It is this tension between unity and diversity to which the Cox Report addressed itself. The balances it proposed are not easy to achieve, and will need continual re-evaluation. We were attacked by the Right Wing who want stability and unity based on the hegemony imposed by the upper and middle classes in the 1930s and before. We were attacked by the Left Wing because we advocated that all children should study Shakespeare and the literature of the past, our English inheritance, and that they should speak and write Standard English. I am unrepentant. British society in the 1990s must develop this balance between unity and diversity. This should be the aim of all political parties; it should be the aim of all teachers of English.

2 The language of organizational change in higher education. Language and social values: the tentacular roots of organizational cultures

DIANA F. DAVIS

Introduction: the parameters of change in Australia

As we contemplate the current context of massive change in Australia and its educational system, we are forced to recognize that these changes have been brought about primarily by economic forces:

- the increasing lack of competitiveness for Australian industry;
- the fact of declining markets for Australian primary products;
- Australia's apparently ever-increasing overseas debt;
- rising unemployment, exceeding 10 per cent, especially for school-leavers and young people;
- the reduction in our international credit rating;
- a declining standard of living for the majority of the population.

Australia's educational output, moreover, has been meagre by comparison with that of other developed nations. Although an increasing number of the 16–24-year-old cohort is continuing in education, the percentage of degrees awarded in technology disciplines is only 5.8 compared with 19.4 in Japan, 9.7 in Germany, and 9.4 in the UK (1987 data). Likewise, the number of engineers per 1000 manufacturing employees is only seven for Australia compared with 70 for the USA and 140 for Japan.

The directions are towards an increasingly bleak future for the school-leaver of the 1990s. The transition to the workplace or to higher education is more problematic than at any time in the past fifty years, given the reality that, unless dramatic change can be wrought in the system and in the economy, a large proportion of the school-leavers of the 1990s will never hold a permanent job.

The combination and imperative of these and other factors have given rise to a new economic rationalism which has indelibly impacted on education, and has seen rhetoric and policy clearly establish a nexus between improved educational performance and Australia's long-term prosperity. This nexus has created change in many aspects of organization, perhaps the most notable being the wholesale restructuring of the tertiary education system and calls for curriculum change at all levels of education.

Equally important, however, is the realization for those in the education industry that the gameboard on which we have been playing for the past thirty years – with its concerns for social values, equity, quality of life issues, etc., and with its very protective rule system – has also been inexorably changed. The external stakeholders – government, employers, parents – will play an increasingly dominant role; the *'we are the professionals'* approach which we, as educators, have employed to build a protective barrier to external interference in *our* determination of our goals, strategies and achievements, has been thoroughly and effectively challenged from above and below. We must learn to play by new rules in this era of economic rationalism. We must learn a new repertoire of behaviour.

Identifying the signs

This is an unprecedented era of change in education and, while some of us may grimace at the idea of marketing expertise and education, we do so at our peril – because behind the rhetoric there is, indeed, real change occurring – and at an increasing pace. Some of the more obvious and immediate signs of this *economic rationalism* in education have been the emergence of:

- a new language;
- a new approach to educational management;
- new values;
- new goals;
- a whole new concern for *output*.

External and corporate influences have impacted significantly on the autonomy of the educational system at all levels – even under essentially socialist governments.

Thus far, the changes have been most evident at the level of the education framework or structure – the contours and shape of education have been altered – new hills, new valleys, new pathways. As yet, however, the changes wrought on the framework have not been fully wrought on the people or fabric of the system. Here, change will be slower and its direction less predictable, but no less inevitable!

As we review the changes in the organizational structures, it is clear that the areas of most significant impact are, firstly **management**, secondly in terms of **goals and values** and thirdly, the **language and communicative structures** which mediate the first two.

Management

We are increasingly adopting the process and procedures of *strategic planning* and *operational management* as constructed and followed in the corporate world. From central administration at government ministry level to university vice-chancellors to heads of schools we are learning to assess our current situation, determine our mission/policy, determine our goals – and then to move towards operationalizing our objectives, choosing appropriate implementation strategies, assessing output/throughput and evaluation. At one level this seems logical, but for many the introduction of a concept such as strategic management heralds a new and alien set of values and goals, and a consequent unwelcome need to learn a new language.

Goals and values

We are being required to justify the value of education, not for its own sake, but as the profession's input into the development of a prosperous, independent and fulfilled nation. We are being forced to take stock of our role in determining the quality of the 'human resource' with significant pragmatic and vocational issues. We are thus confronted by the question as to what we, as educators, are doing to help the nation fulfil its destiny and to meet the worldly aspirations of its people. Increasingly, there is the acknowledgement that, in this new age of the communication society, school and university must play a significant part in developing new skills, abilities and values.

As has been widely acknowledged, the 'Fordist' society with the dependent, non-thinking worker who could 'park his brains' at the door of his place of employment has disappeared. So, too, has the era when teachers and educators could regard the future ability/skill/intellectual requirements demanded by employers as not their responsibility. While some may protest that it was never really like that, it is clear now that we are to be accountable for what we do with our students' time and our part of the taxation dollar.

Language and communicative structures

Not only has the language changed; there have been accompanying fundamental changes to our communicative structures. At the level of vocabulary the winds of change have brought to the educational landscape numerous examples of new language – terms and concepts such as:

- strategic management;
- mission or policy statement;

- profiles;
- programme budgets and budgeting;
- zero-based budgeting;
- performance indicators;
- performance appraisal;
- quality and effectiveness;
- through-put rates;
- marketing;
- accountability;

and the like. This language signposts the changes, and at the same time challenges our established patterns of thought and behaviour. We must not ignore the reality that, 'As lawyers know only too well, and as political scientists continue to ignore, public policy is made of language. Whether as text or talk, discourse is central in all stages of the policy process' (Agar, 1987: 113).

Moreover, 'when management chooses a particular organization form, it is providing not only a framework for current operations but also channels along which strategic information will flow' (Bower, 1970: 287). Pocock (1984) refers to 'verbalization itself as a political act' and asserts the need to 'start with a consideration of words as actions and as acts of power towards persons' (Pocock, 1984: 26). Using as his exemplar Brutus's soliloquy presaging the murder of Caesar in Shakespeare's *Julius Caesar*,

> Between the acting of a dreadful thing
> And the first motion, all the interim is
> Like a phantasma or a hideous dream.
>   (*Julius Caesar*, II, i, 63–65)

he concludes that:

> Verbalizations, we now see, act upon people – and so constitute acts of power – in at least two ways: either by informing them and so modifying their perceptions or by defining them and so modifying the ways in which they are perceived by others. Either of these acts of power may be entirely unilateral and arbitrary: performed, that is, by the will of one person only. (Pocock, 1984: 28)

Shuy (1987: 44) makes the point that:

> All speakers have strategies for advancing their own agendas and, conversely, for ignoring, blocking, or thwarting the agendas of others, especially those agendas with which they are not comfortable. It is in this area of conversational strategies, especially strategies which block the agendas of the other speaker, where recent government practice causes concern.

His database enabled him to identify seven types of conversational power:

1. The power of known conversational significance.
2. The power of controlled agenda.

3. The power of camouflaged agenda.
4. The power of created atmosphere.
5. The power of blocked agenda.
6. The power of conversational isolation.
7. The power of deliberately unclear language use.

(Ibid, 1987: 44)

Furthermore Fairclough (1989) argues that: 'Unprecedented state and institutional control (specifically by "public" institutions) is exercised over individuals through various forms of bureaucracy.' The 'colonization of people's lives' through such bureaucratic controls, he points out, is achieved through the salience of 'strategic discourse, discourse oriented to instrumental goals, to getting results' (Fairclough, 1989: 198). For individuals whose orientation is towards Habermas's (1984) 'communicative discourse, which is oriented to reaching understanding between participants', the experience of dissonance between usual and preferred types of discourse could create dysfunction and a barrier to change.

Current educational cultures

For this reason it is important to examine current educational cultures at the people or 'human resource' level, as well as how this structural change is managed at the system level. Government-perceived imperatives can, of course, be realized in structures which in and of themselves can be seen to be desirable in achieving outcomes in financial and efficiency terms. However, for such structural change to achieve realization at the educational operations level, it must also involve the human resource which carries out the operations – and that human resource must be mobilized towards achievement of those goals. Consequently, it is pertinent to examine current educational cultures with a view to identifying characteristic patterns and mores, especially in relation to communication – for it is through the use of language that people adapt to and accept their role in making change work or, alternatively, react negatively to and, hence, work to resist change.

Barbara Kovach (1989) in her important analysis of *The Organizational Gameboard* reminds us that:

From the late 1940s through the early 1970s, pyramids – the pyramidal form – established the unspoken roles for corporate, for profit organizations, while circles – the circular form – established the rules for educational, governmental, not for profit organizations. The rules of the pyramid or the rules of the circle were learned slowly over time by employees within these institutions and, often, the rules served them well over a lifetime. They [the employees] did not know that they were rules but rather 'just the way things were'.   (Kovach, 1989: vii)

In Kovach's (1989) terms:

Effective circles are characterized by openness, warmth, and responsiveness to individuals . . .

> Effective pyramids are characterized by efficiency, briskness, and a sense that
> things are happening.   (Kovach, 1989: 29)

What we have now, of course, is that the values of the pyramidal structure have been firmly imported, virtually by edict, into the arena into which circles have traditionally operated. As language and literacy experts we have predominantly valued the circular model of exploratory talk rather than language to get things done (Britton, 1971). Exploratory talk values and protects the ideas of the group. As Kovach (1989) points out 'Circles . . . are the flat systems in organizations in which all members are relatively equal'. In education we have operated over the past twenty years in structures which have valued openness and democracy – participative decision-making has been an overt goal of the system, but as I have argued elsewhere, 'The organizational demands of a new era of change render this less appropriate as the context often requires decisive action from doers rather than talkers.'

Cardinal Newman, in his treatise *The Idea of a University*, draws an analogy with:

> . . . practised travellers, when they first come into a place, mounting some high
> hill or church tower, by way of reconnoitring its neighbourhood. In like manner
> you must be above your knowledge . . . not under it, or it will oppress you; and
> the more you have of it the greater will be the load . . . in every case, to
> command it is to mount above it.   (1873: 117)

We need to think about Newman's notion that, 'In every case, to command it is to mount above it' and consider its implications for our language behaviour. Most people take their language behaviour for granted; even people sensitized to the nuances of language behaviour can fail to reflect on their own language. Wright Mills has drawn some interesting distinctions between personal and institutional contexts in this regard:

> Conversation may be concerned with the factual features of a situation as they
> are seen or believed to be or it may seek to integrate and promote a set of
> diverse social actions with reference to the situation and its normative patterns
> of expectations. It is in this latter assent and dissent phase of conversation that
> persuasive and dissuasive speech and vocabulary arise. For men live in immedi-
> ate acts of experience and their attentions are directed outside themselves until
> acts are in some way frustrated. It is then that awareness of self and of motive
> occur.   (Wright Mills, 1984: 14)

> Men discern situations with particular vocabularies, and it is in terms of some
> delimited vocabulary that they anticipate consequences of conduct . . . Institu-
> tionally different situations have different *vocabularies of motive* appropriate
> to their respective behaviors.   (Wright Mills, 1984: 15)

Extrapolating from Newman (1915), it may well be the capacity to command both internal and external reflections of self and context which helps individuals to cope with change.

Empowerment of the human resource: language as facilitator or inhibitor

As researchers and educators concerned with language as an essentially human resource we are also necessarily concerned with the role of language in the empowerment of individuals in a whole range of contexts at micro- and macro-levels. Except in rare instances, humans live in and move between a range of interlocking, interdependent and yet identifiably different group interactional structures. Language is thus the dominant communicative strategy of the human resource:

> Without it we could not symbolize: reason, remember, anticipate, rationalize, distort, and evoke beliefs and perceptions about matters not immediately before us. With it we not only describe reality but create our own realities, which take forms that overlap with each other and may not be mutually consistent. When it suits us to see rationalization as reason, repression as help, distortion as creation, or the converse of any of these, language and mind can smoothly structure each other to do so . . . When the complicated problems involve social power and status, distortion and misperception are virtually certain to occur.
>
> (Edelman, 1984: 45)

One general level of differentiation between human interactional groups is related to purpose – personal, familial, relational, recreational or professional. In a sense, the *professional* stands apart from the others because, whether you are a waste disposal operative or a corporate executive, you achieve your major interaction with external societal structure(s) through that professional position – and that interaction affects, to a greater or lesser extent, all of your other group affiliations. As an individual you have the power to change many of your other affiliations: you can resign from a tennis club or as the treasurer of the drama society. You can change a personal relationship by withdrawing and, indeed, much of the control you exercise in changing or modifying these affiliations is exercised through language. By contrast, at the professional level, control is rarely as much within the ambit of the individual, especially if that professional relationship exists within the framework of corporate or government enterprise, in which any individual is but a part of what is increasingly referred to as the 'human resource' – a resource now considered at least as powerful and significant in its role as the physical or fiscal resources which have so much been the focus, in the past, of management concern.

However, whilst modern management practice recognizes the vital significance of the 'human resource', we are still a long way from understanding or establishing effective strategies for ensuring that the human resource is able, not only to contemplate and project change, but also to respond to it and manage it in a way which leads to effective growth and improved productivity. We are even further from understanding the many ways – some incredibly subtle – in which written and oral language motivates or inhibits that human resource in a time of change.

Frederickson and Mitchell have introduced the concept of comprehensiveness, which encompasses the human resource element in strategic management in terms of 'the extent to which organizations attempt to be exhaustive or inclusive in making and integrating strategic decisions' (Frederickson, 1984: 445). As a result of a subsequent study Frederickson (1984) stresses the importance of recognizing that:

> participation in the strategic process is not limited to a few individuals who are located at the very top of the organization. Although final choice may be the prerogative of a single individual, numerous authors (Carter, 1971; Chandler, 1962; Quinn, 1980) have recognized that individuals at a variety of locations and levels throughout the organization participate in information gathering and processing activities. Therefore, [he says], it is the patterned behaviour of these individuals that makes one organization's strategic process highly comprehensive, while another is very non-comprehensive . . . [and, consequently, in order] to understand the comprehensiveness construct as an organization level phenomenon, one must understand what it means for individuals' decision-making behavior, and how that behavior becomes patterned.
>
> (Frederickson, 1984: 459–60)

However, Frederickson does not make the logical connection between language, communication structures and decision-making behaviour.

Levels of the implementation/operational process

The systemic level

The strategic management of change, of course, occurs at a number of levels – most notably the system level, secondly the specific organization level and, thirdly, structural levels at which individuals function within the organization. There has been significant systemic level change in the Australian higher education sector since 1988. As an educator within that system, and one exposed to at least some of the managerial challenges of that change, there has been plenty of impetus, if not a great deal of leisure, to reflect on its strategic management. The major change is the creation of the 'Unified National System' of Higher Education outlined briefly below.

Australia had in place for many years a range of higher education institutions – in common with both Britain and North America where a diversity of post-secondary paths also prevailed. Latterly in Australia, this was referred to as the 'binary system', regarded by government as quintessentially problematic and in urgent need of disbandment. Thus, a 'Green Paper' appeared early in 1988, which turned into a 'White' or policy paper by July 1988. Institutions were urged to seek amalgamations, small with big so that big became bigger. Small was definitely not beautiful – and there were also financial push factors as an imperative to action. With hindsight, what were the parameters of the strategic management process by which Australia's tertiary institutions were reduced from 70 to 45 (38 is the target) by the end of 1990 leaving but a few institutions poised on, or alternatively withdrawing from the brink of amalgamation at the beginning of 1991?

The Green Paper indicated that the government would welcome views from the higher education community on 'practical options for change' by the end of April 1988. Given that the period from mid-December to early February spanned the long vacation peak summer period for tertiary institutions when most academics seek to take their annual vacation, the discussion period timing was less generous than it might initially appear.

The language of the invitation to participate in the discussion phase – views on practical options for change – is significant. The use of the term 'view' with its connotations of opinion set the scene for a gathering of opinions which have no status beyond that and, indeed, connote self-interest by the very use of the term. The delimiting of 'views' to 'practical options for change' implies that even views about 'no change' are not part of the agenda. What I am suggesting, then, is that language – and the presentation of that language in a spatial and visual format – plays a critical role in the strategic management process; yet it is a role which has been barely recognized by the literature.

Part I of the Green Paper, entitled *Assessing the Challenge*, examines four areas. The first 'The Nature of the Challenge' identifies issues of concern to the government – the general unreality and uncertainty of the contemporary world; the rising ambiguity of Australia's traditional principal export bases; labour gluts at the unskilled end and shortages at the other; the under-representation in higher education of disadvantaged groups; likely atrophy and inefficiency in the higher education system. The argument is that an expanded and reformed higher education system will ameliorate these problems.

The second chapter, 'The Size of the Task' purports to examine the potential for growth in the present system and to identify potential shortfalls. Chapter 3 requests institutions to consider a range of academic and non-academic issues including admission standards, course length and content, bridging arrangements and attrition rates, etc. The fourth is entitled 'A Fair Chance for All' and emphasizes equality of educational opportunity. By its white reincarnation as a policy document, Part I was called *The Environment for Reform* and simply had two chapters entitled 'The Context' and 'Growth and Equity'. The other three parts were as follows – and the agenda is implicit in the blunt titles:

Part II – The Unified National System.
Part III – The Allocation of Resources.
Part IV – Organizational Effectiveness.

How does such systemic dogma translate at the institutional level?

The institutional level

At the institutional level such written reports are variously summarized, typically also in written form. One institution provided the essence of the White Paper's (Commonwealth Government of Australia, 1988) vision of the Unified National System in this statement published for all staff in the university's broadsheet and reflecting the edict-like quality of the original:

> The system will consist of a range of higher education institutions with specific missions agreed with, and funded by, the Commonwealth. Diversity and quality are paramount; it will not be a uniform system. Teaching will remain the predominant activity of all institutions, whereas research will vary according to demonstrated capacity.
>
> No institution will be guaranteed funding for research across all its fields of study. Institutions which decide to remain outside the unified national system will have no guaranteed base of Commonwealth funding and will be funded by contract for specified teaching activities.
>
> All institutions are invited to apply for membership of the unified national system before the end of September 1988. The final determination of membership will be made by the end of 1988. This application will require an initial commitment in the areas of internal management, credit transfer, staffing arrangements, a common academic year and equity . . .
>
> Profile-based funding arrangements will apply to all institutions in 1989, but from 1990 only to those within the national system.
>
> (Monash University, 1988)

Very much a pyrrhic invitation! Yet a fiscal imperative is always a compelling one to management. As institutional leaders made the requisite moves on behalf of their respective institutions either to become bigger by acquisition or to survive by being acquired, the oral discourse at the human resource level developed a whole new range of greeting pleasantries: 'What institution are *you* hopping into bed with this week?' 'Did you hear that X College is making overtures to V University?'

While individuals may attempt to reflect control over their fears through such jocular references, they also serve to denigrate the process and vitiate the power of government goals – probably a fairly unavoidable consequence of implementation by edict (Nutt, 1989). The interplay of individuals' skills, expertise, power, influence, needs, aspirations – and capacity to use language – becomes very important in a process of change which requires commitment at all levels of the strategic process.

The individual level

The capacity of the individual to behave in ways which are not only potentially or actively unhelpful to the organization but also to the individual
must be a matter for concern. Varenne (1987) has suggested that:

> Social interaction may always be a matter of individual egoisms struggling to
> achieve their goals in ways that are barely 'mitigated'.   (Varenne, 1987: 130)

In an era where, to use the common parlance, disparate tertiary institutions
are forced to become bedfellows, an individual's capacity and willingness
'to read the Handwriting on the Wall', as Bell (1988) expresses it, becomes
critical.

Staff development strategies – the new corporate mediator of change –
must be sensitive to the discourse of the players. Performance appraisal, for
example, is very much integral to the strategic process – but how much do
we know about its parameters and effectiveness? A cornerstone of its current
implementation is counselling by supervisors. Yet, in examining the relationship between the organizational feedback environment and performance,
Becker and Klimoski (1989) are critical of the limited research in the area,
arguing that:

> The majority of these studies involve isolated instances of feedback presentation
> and a single criterion of performance, and many of them take place in a labora-
> tory setting.   (Becker and Klimoski, 1989: 343)

They go on to point out that:

> The major dimensions of feedback studied to date have been the source, sign,
> and amount/frequency of feedback.   (Becker and Klimoski, 1989: 343)

Their study found that 'the Negative Expressions and Positive Job Change
factors [were] more related to performance than the other organizational/
supervisory factors' (Becker and Klimoski, 1989: 356). This finding prompted
them to pose the question:

> Why should negative expressions from the organization/supervisor be directly
> (and negatively) related to performance but negative consequences from this
> source be only indirectly related to performance?
>   (Becker and Klimoski, 1989: 356)

Their exploration of possible and plausible explanations does not include
the possibility that negative expressions from someone in a supervisory role
may be more disheartening and harder to take than negative consequences –
such as being unsuccessful in promotion or in rejection for a more senior
position – and that language plays a key role in such response patterns.

Language as mediator of the strategic management process

Language is the key dynamic force in the utilization and development of the human resource and plays a central role in mediating the strategic management process. This role can be, on the one hand, a powerful force for innovation, development and improvement, *or* on the other, an equally powerful force for the 'status quo' or for the 'head in the sand' – for stagnation and for failure.

March and Simon (1958) suggest that organizational structures serve a primary function in providing bounds of rationality which transcend the cognitive limitations of individuals. While we do not, at this stage, fully understand the role of language in strategic management and decision-making, we do know that decision-making is not solely dependent on rationality. Language clearly plays a critical and not necessarily conventionally rational role in the change process – especially the role of oracy as a mediator between the *precept or principle*, most often promulgated through the traditional literacy's written form, and the *practice* which tends to be most effectively disseminated by word of mouth.

It is not just a truism that 'Bureaucracy . . . breaks apart substance from appearances, action from responsibility, and language from meaning' (Jackall, 1983: 130), but a reality of practice. The written word promulgates bureaucracy which, in the practice, thus 'makes its own internal rules and social context the principal moral gauges for action' (Jackall, 1983: 130).

In a recent issue of the *Strategic Management Journal*, Montgomery *et al.* (1989) commented that:

> strategy research, in our judgement, has had surprisingly little impact on practice. In fact, the influence has tended to flow in the opposite direction, where practice invents, and teaching disseminates.   (Montgomery *et al.*, 1989: 194)

In education we have observed the same phenomenon.

These authors do not devote their attention to hypothesizing about why this might be so, but tend rather to advance excuses – 'strategy is a young field' – and to moot instead their suggestions for change. From a rather different perspective, Bateman and Zeithaml (1989), in their study of the psychological context of strategic decisions, however, do cite a number of studies in support of their hypothesis that:

> The decision-making process is dependent not only on objective information and rationality, but also on decision-makers' cognitions about the world.
>
>   (Bateman and Zeithaml, 1989: 69)

They acknowledge, indeed, that:

> Although decision feedback, perceived slack, and other aspects of the decision context may provide the background conditions for important managerial

decisions, the language and labels employed during the decision process may influence the way in which decision-makers respond to these conditions.

(Bateman and Zeithaml, 1989: 70)

The language of governmental edict in our context tends always to be written. The current Australian Government's strategy is to produce 'Green Papers' which are promulgated for discussion after which they are proclaimed as 'White Paper' policy. Cynics says that white papers are green papers which have been photocopied – a reflection perhaps of the degree of movement perceived to have taken place after the discussion phase.

We all know of the inherent differences between speech and writing:

> The nature of truth and reality that we expect in face-to-face conversation is different from what we expect in writing ... Words as spoken are typically reduced, slurred, run together, or even purposely ambiguous. Their meaning is mediated by how they are spoken. When written, words are discrete, definite, and committed. (Tannen, 1987: 4–5)

What is perhaps less recognized is what happens to written edicts as they are constructed into the human resource's scope of implementation. If we argue that:

> All speech ... is performative in the sense that it does things to people [and to written texts by redefining] ... them in their own perceptions, in those of others and by restructuring the conceptual universes in which they are perceived. (Pocock, 1984: 39)

It is clear that oral language is the key mediator in the strategic management process. If we return to Kovach's (1989) organizational gameboard and examine the various players' orientation vis-à-vis the strategic planning and management tasks, we will see that talk plays a critical role.

If the oral mediation remains within the realm of *communicative* discourse and does not move towards the goals of *strategic* discourse there is a potentially major problem for the organization. I would hypothesize that it is the travellers who are most likely to achieve that transition. It probably does not matter greatly in a time of no change or very slow change whether an organization has predominantly hill dwellers (those who work best in pyramid structures) or valley dwellers (those who work best in circles). In a time of rapid change, however, this becomes not only important, but critical. Faced with change, Kovach (1989) observes that the hill dwellers tend to stand alone against the change while the valley dwellers huddle together in a circle. Although hill and valley dwellers use different coping strategies both groups operate in the hope that the change will go away.

If change is to be effected within organizations and structures, however, neither the hill dwellers nor the valley dwellers can accomplish it alone. It is essential to have travellers to make it work because they alone recognize the inherent values of the approaches of both the hill and the valley dwellers, and hence are able to mediate forward solutions. They alone are able to see the need for the valley dwellers' participatory strategies in reaching decisions about new directions, as well as the need for the hill dwellers' skills in translating these new missions into action and results.

Managing the tentacles

The central theme of Kedar's (1987) book *Power Through Discourse* is 'that language-use plays a critical role in the attainment and/or exercise of power', although she acknowledges that:

> the ability to achieve and maintain power is not solely an outcome of language use [given that] nonlinguistic social factors such as network systems, physical coercion, the ability to gather and use information effectively, and so on, all figure in political and negotiative success.   (Kedar, 1987: v)

Language and communicative structures are central to the effective implementation of strategic planning. Governments and organizations which ignore this reality will do so at the ultimate peril of their policies and plans.

3 From production to deployment: talking and writing for social action

PETER MEDWAY

Two uses of writing

English teachers use all sorts of formal and informal schemes to distinguish the different sorts of written and spoken language they want their students to experience, but one basic distinction is seldom made. I can illustrate it with two pieces of writing, by students of the same age (14–15), but from different schools and different subject lessons. The first, of which I print only the opening and a later section, is by Joanne from Breeze Hill School in Oldham, Lancashire.

> *The less fortunate people*
> It all began with 2 social workers – Earl and John – coming to school, and talking to us about the Arthur and Kenyon Centre, on Wellyhole Street.
>
> Before John and Earl came to talk to us, we thought of the people who attended the centre as aliens, probably because we were a little bit scared of them, because they're different, and we didn't understand, but after listening to what John and Earl had to say, I became interested in the centre, and wanted to know more about these mentally dis-abled people – who are really no different than ourselves.
>
> Five of us went up to the A&K Centre that first Friday morning, and were immediately greeted by about 20 people – all mentally handicapped, each trying to hold our hands, or show us in some other way we were welcome.
>
> I now realise that touch is a very important part of communication – as alot of the people who attend the centre, are deaf or don't understand sign language . . .

The project Developing English for TVEI was funded by the Training Agency of the UK Employment Department and was based in the University of Leeds from 1989 to 1990. The report of the project, *Developing English for TVEI* (the DEFT Report), by J. Brown, S. Clarke, P. Medway, and A. Stibbs, with R. Andrews, is obtainable free of charge from TVEI Enquiry Point, MEADS, PO Box 12, Nottingham NG7 2GB, quoting TVEI Reference No. R23.

The second writer is a student in the fourth year (year 10 in the new terminology), so that the '5th years' addressed are a year older.

> 5th years please could you paint all the radiators and pipes Green (undercoat) Please paint notice board (sand gold emulsion paint) and coat hangers as well. Can you also paint the shelves left of the door green When you have finish with the paints and brushes can you put them back in the box
> P.S. please paint rim of notice board green.
> Thanks
> PPPS make sure brushes are completley clean, and make a good job of it.

The first sort of writing, although not traditionally associated with English, is becoming increasingly familiar as English teachers learn to tap the intense experiences gained by students in work and community placements. In several other respects, too, the writing would sit happily inside the typical year 10 or year 11 English folder in the UK and other systems. First, it was produced in response to a demand for writing for the purposes of a school subject. Second, it is a standalone piece which does not depend on readers' knowledge of the context of its production; we can read it in another time and place without difficulty and, moreover, without violating the spirit in which it was written. It was, in fact, in a sense written for us or for anyone; at any rate, it partially complies with the conventions of communicating with an anonymous public audience.

Third, it represents an experience through a narrative which emphasizes 'interiority' (what it was like to be the writer having the experience), but also passes easily into generalization (about what the writer has learned). As often with such writing, it is hard to know how far the attitudes are being shaped with a view to securing approval. Few teachers, however, read the piece as merely an exercise in cynical manipulation and (the fourth point) the educational claim seems plausible that the writing performs for the writer a function beyond mere task-compliance, that of enabling her to go over the experience again in a reflective or celebratory spirit. Joanne seems to do fresh work on her recollections, ideas and attitudes, as well as fulfilling a communicative demand.

If this is right, the piece will have served a purpose even if nobody reads it (although at the same time it is unlikely to have been written had there been no prospect of an audience). Moreover, besides the writer's reflective need having been met, a complete transaction has, even before any reading, been enacted, namely the production on demand of a piece of reflective representation. Although subsequent reading and response by an audience would enhance the value of the experience for the student, they would be a bonus.

It seems reasonable to attach the label 'literary' to texts which display these features: that is, which are produced as instances of writing, in contexts where such manifestations are sought; which are self-contained; which convey the nature of subjective experience; which address a potentially wide and unknown audience; which appear to perform some heuristic function for the writer; and the accomplishment of which completes a transaction.

The second piece is less easy to place. It, too, was produced in a lesson, in a subject called Agriculture/Horticulture; what the fifth years were to paint was the animal house. Although it would not go into a folder to be assessed as part of a public examination process, the text was an outcome of the official curriculum, since in this school, under the Technical and Vocational Education Initiative (TVEI – of which more later), the purpose of the Agriculture/Horticulture course had been redefined as learning to run an enterprise (in this case a smallholding) rather than acquiring applied biological knowledge.

There are other points of contrast. While one student physically wrote this second piece, he or she (I do not know which) wrote on behalf of three students, two female and one male. Moreover, it does not matter which of them it was, since no part of the purpose of the writing was the expression of individuality. More importantly for my purpose, the note is not a standalone artefact. Although broadly intelligible to readers in other times and places (though you would not have known which radiators were being referred to or who the fifth years were), the writing does not work outside the context of its production. For the writing of the note, unlike that of Joanne's piece, represents not the completion of a transaction, but its initiation. What still has to happen is a response to the request, in the form of painting, brush-cleaning and so on, or a refusal to help. The genre is essentially 'request for action: action', and not 'demand for writing: writing' (see Ann Friedman, in Reid, 1987). Without the response from the fifth years the writing will have been useless. What is more, it will have no further use after the response, having entirely served its purpose (and, in fact, the note was thrown away, to survive for our perusal only because of my researcher colleague's magpie instincts). Our present reading of the note, thus, falls right outside the intentions of the writer in producing it.

English and the language of participation

The distinction I want to emphasize is that between a language performance which completes a transaction (for instance, by fulfilling a demand for writing) and one which instigates a further performance, verbal or non-verbal: on the one hand, language with no expectation of real world consequences other than a reading or readings; on the other, language with intended consequences in the world of actions.

English has almost exclusively been about the first sort of language performance. Students write within literary genres, to reflect and celebrate, and to learn to produce satisfactory instances of the genre; and they talk to exchange experience and reflect on it, to arrive at versions of the world and to make sense of literary texts. Any language for affecting action has been fictional, embedded within those literary genres: only in novels, stories and plays do students generally gain sanctioned experience of the linguistic performatives of haggling, ordering, pleading, sentencing, lovemaking, warning and threatening.

There is a case, which I will not argue here, but simply refer to and identify myself with, that such a curriculum, rich though it is when viewed in contrast with what it supplanted, is impoverished when judged in terms of the distinction I have made here, and that English needs to give a more prominent place to language with intended consequences in the world of action. The main reasons for this belief are that the world mainly runs on such language, so that students need to acquire competence in it, and that process can provide an alternative route towards general linguistic competences, with different motivations and facilitations.

It was this argument about English that informed the project which I now proceed to describe. A group of us in the Universities of Leeds and Hull and in a number of schools and local education authorities (LEAs) wanted to try out an English curriculum which would get students using language to affect states of affairs. The opportunity came with funding from a government initiative which aimed to give all 14–18-year-old full-time students an adequate vocational preparation, the TVEI already referred to. ('Vocational' was very broadly interpreted; it was not the intention to train students for specific jobs.) Preparation for working life includes preparation for participation in contexts of action, which in turn involves what I have called language with intended consequences. 'The language of participation' became part of the jargon of our project, which we called Developing English for TVEI, or DEFT.

The twenty or so colleagues who joined us from ten schools and five LEAs undertook, in return for nothing more than travel expenses and funded supply cover for project meetings, to develop two units of year 10 or 11 work per school, each to last several weeks. These projects, in the event, included producing marketing and publicity materials for local enterprises, community newspapers and children's stories for specific needs; conducting research and producing recommendations for a school librarian; promoting personal safety in a local area; evaluating care facilities; investigating school leavers' experiences; and exchanging students between schools.

The ways in which such projects would entail direct participation in affairs rather than modes such as fact-finding and reporting, which are already well known in school, are admittedly not obvious; indeed, I will later suggest that interesting forms of immediate engagement remain to be explored. The language of participation was, however, extensively experienced by students in the process of organizing and managing the operations. (I will also explain later that such experience was not limited to that area.) Brief descriptions of two projects will illustrate the nature of the students' language experience.

Work in two schools

Counthill School is an 11–18 comprehensive school in Oldham. A requirement of Helen Lennie's TVEI English post was to work with Bob Moxam,
the newly appointed teacher responsible for developing technology across the
curriculum. Helen and her head of English, Dave Garnett, conceived the
idea that year 10 English students might help Bob ascertain the impact of
technology on staff and students in the school. Thus, Dave's and Helen's
classes (a high ability and a middle ability set), working together, conducted
numerous inquiries amongst teachers, other staff and students. Topics
included students' perceptions of technology as an optional or elective
subject, female students' experience of that subject, access to hardware,
heads of departments' views of the place of technology in the school, and the
impact of technology on the school administration. The results were written
up and word-processed, and then, because the LEA saw the utility of the
document and supplied funding, printed as a spiral-bound report for distri-
bution to teachers and administrators across the city.

The demand on the students for the effective use of a language of participation arose from the complexity and openness of the operation. Within the
unit of 60 students (and not the usual 30) more separate activities were going
on than could be closely monitored. Because of the number and interlocking
nature of the decisions required, only the most general control could be
exercised by the teachers, so that students were forced to take responsibility
on themselves, and to consult with each other and reach agreement. Such
were the logistical demands on Helen and Dave that students who *wished*
to put the onus of decision-making back onto them would often have a
long wait to get their attention. All this negotiation, arguing, planning and
co-ordinating provided extended experience of language with intended
consequences.

A project from a second school was similarly based on inquiry. In the
words of Malcolm Kirtley, the teacher at Hayfield School, Doncaster:

> The aim of the project was to survey a range of careers around the Doncaster
> area and write a series of critical case studies. These would be put together in a
> casebook which would be for an audience of fourth or fifth year students actu-
> ally to use, and we would try to get it placed in the careers library in town. We
> had looked at some of the existing casebooks used to give the kids an awareness
> of careers, and they were incredibly boring documents written by PR people.

The heart of the inquiry process would be interviewing. Malcolm was concerned that the students going into workplaces should be resourceful and
flexible interviewers, 'so that they could improvise if certain areas developed,
they could pursue them and would not simply sit with their heads down on
this piece of paper, scribbling things down; there would be an interaction.'
He therefore organized two practice stages in which the students interviewed
first their parents and then teachers, and evaluated each experience. Here,

too, a great deal of language of participation was involved, especially in organizing the interviews.

I now want to indicate in a more general way the sorts of language experience which the DEFT activities made possible, taking oral and written language in turn.

Oral language experience

Teachers found that DEFT activities promoted confident and articulate talk, particularly where students found themselves in an authoritative expert role. Oral activities included planning, decision-making, editing, organizing and managing with peers in small and large groups, and in formal and informal meetings; teaching technical skills to peers; discussion of experiences and findings; seeking help from teachers and negotiating with them for release, equipment, etc.; interviewing adults in numerous roles, in and out of school; using the telephone to seek information and help, and to negotiate arrangements; communicating with adults while accompanying them, sometimes over long periods, at work; making, transcribing and analysing tape recordings; and making oral presentations (e.g. launching a brochure, bidding for a contract).

Written language experience

(1) Ephemeral

Much writing produced as a by-product of students' ongoing participation in a collaborative enterprise was purely instrumental and had no value for the participants once its function had been discharged. Such texts tended to be brief, uninteresting in their 'internal' features and intelligible only in part to those not privy to the context; hence they tended to get lost. They included notes made during interviews, in the analysis of interviews, in planning, and in taking down information over the telephone; memos and letters (e.g. requesting equipment, requesting an interview, requesting help and thanking), and minutes of decision-making meetings. Students had to learn unfamiliar aspects of writerly capability, such as deciding when to write: should a letter or memo, for instance, precede, follow or serve instead of a spoken communication?

What the students learned had to do less with the forms and conventions of texts than with their uses in getting things done. For instance, students discovered that writing was often the only way to get through to the 'right quarters' in situations of organizational complexity. In both Counthill and Hayfield, requests to busy teachers for interviews, release from lessons and other help had to be written, both to avoid long queues for face-to-face transactions and to enable the teachers to formulate a single coherent response to a range of incoming requests. The necessity became apparent, in other words, for efficient bureaucracy and its literate realization through forms, lists and records, as Shoshona Zuboff (1988) observed:

> As the size of enterprises grew it became increasingly difficult to operate by word of mouth. Written communication was required in order to ensure clarity in both lateral and subordinate relationships. There was a growing need for internal documentation, record keeping, and external correspondence. People and systems were needed to produce, maintain, and access the burgeoning load of written information.

Some texts seen by the students as ephemeral in function, nevertheless, displayed written qualities generally prized by English teachers. This draft of a letter to an ambulance crew was discovered by Malcolm Kirtley amongst rough notes which the writer would shortly have discarded (the final version had been sent):

> Dear Sir,
> A few weeks ago you allowed Daniel Clarke and myself, to visit your station, look around, talk to yourself and your crew. This letter is just to thank you for permitting the visit to take place. It was a great day and the information gained will be very important to the case study I'm involved in.
> The only dissapointment was hearing the news of one of your crew passing away the night before, which I was very sorry to hear about. Despite the sadness, all the people we met showed the true spirit of the ambulance service. You were very friendly, you made us feel very welcome and had a smile when inside you probably didn't feel like smiling.
> The day made me realize that being an ambulance man isn't all glamour but not all blood and guts either, it's having a good personality and really caring for people. It has made me very interested in the job.
> Again I would like to thank you.
> Yours sincerely,
> Mark

An aspect of writing experienced only irregularly in normal English work, but routinely by DEFT students was its occurrence in close association with speech. Functionally, the two may be almost equivalent, as when you tell your colleague the message someone has phoned through or, if she is not at hand, leave a note on her desk. Students also wrote in preparation for speaking and after spoken transactions to make a record or formalize a decision. A further set of skills involved writing connected with interviews, for planning, recording, analysing and reporting. It was good for students to learn that accounts of interviews are not derived unproblematically from the data, but are constructed through a series of value-laden decisions, the language of the account deriving partly from the subject and partly from the writer.

(2) Final product

This category included reports (published and unpublished, general summaries and case studies), accounts of experiences (often for folders to be submitted for public examinations), newspapers, published stories, scripts for acting, leaflets and advice sheets, and publicity materials. Such writing, although not as immediately 'participatory' as the ephemeral memos and lists referred to earlier, differed from the usual written outcomes of English in being directed not only to teachers and peers, but also to other readers, some of whom would put it to practical use. It could display virtuosic literary qualities, like this account of a visit to a solicitor's office by Hayfield student Kate Oldfield:

> . . . On entering Mr Burrow's personal office it was easy to see just how much paperwork was involved. The room was filled with towers of paper in every possible corner. No sooner had we sat down to begin our interview than the phone rang and Mr Burrow was assuring a business associate of some deal or other. He will sometimes take fifty calls a day.
>
> To be a solicitor takes a person who can work under extreme pressure and who has great personal organisation. An image must be projected to the clients of sharp professionalism, Mr Burrow told us. The old-fashioned idea of the solicitor must be discarded; no more walking up endless rickety stairs to a dingy room full of dust and cobwebs. And so Mr Burrow led us up endless rickety stairs to a dingy room full of dust and cobwebs. The shelves of files were eternal and the papers scattered everywhere. We realised that the sharp image of organized professionalism had been left in the plush reception room.

Modes of engagement

One can examine the language of DEFT students in terms of the modes in which they related to their situations. Some students used writing in very much the approved English style as a vehicle for reflection, rehearsal and celebration. Joanne's piece about the centre for adults with learning difficulties is an example. Such writing was often occasioned by the need for assessable work to go in the folder. Although there is a great deal that could be said about this writing, I will confine myself to one observation. In Joanne's school the teachers reported that during work at the centre some students saw for the first time the point of personal and reflective writing, faced as they were with a powerful experience that they felt a need to evaluate and share.

The modes, however, which were more distinctive of DEFT and through which students engaged with 'the significant others' in their work situations, were inquiry and participation. It is worth examining the contexts in which each occurred.

Within the small working groups which planned and ran the inquiries and produced the collaborative final texts, students routinely deployed language

Table 3.1   Modes of engagement

Mode of communicative involvement	With fellow students	With 'target' groups
Inquiry	n/a	Yes
Participation	Yes	No

with intent to affect the state of affairs: organizing, negotiating, cajoling, refusing, suggesting, ordering and so on. Verbal formulations were generated and uttered within the situations which the speakers wanted to affect, so that production and deployment were one, and feedback was immediate from observation of the effect induced: the job taken on or refused by a co-worker, the scissors passed, the cut agreed, the typeface selected.

In immediate dealings with outsiders, on the other hand, the language used was primarily one of inquiry: essentially, the students asked questions. These linguistic engagements, though certainly interactive, did not have the purpose of bringing about action or changing intentions.

There was, thus, an apparent asymmetry in the students' experience of the two modes. It can be represented as in Table 3.1, where 'Participation' is a form of engagement meant to have an effect on the state of affairs – to change it or maintain it.

One could justifiably argue, therefore, that the need remains for ex-periments by English teachers in getting their students into an actively *participative* mode with groups outside the school, instead of just an inquiry mode (discussed further in Medway, 1991). In fact, DEFT did throw up at least one clear example of this, the Breeze Hill project, in which students worked with adults as co-actors in the Centre. To conclude with an emphasis on unfinished business, however, would be unfair and misleading, for two reasons: first, 'participation' occurred in less obvious ways, not noted above, which it is important to recognize; and, second, the crude dichotomy I have set up between inquiry and participation needs considerable qualification.

On the first point we may note that 'inquiry' with people outside the school can only get under way once all sorts of arrangements and agreements have been made. Where, as in DEFT, it is the students who are responsible for these negotiations, 'language with intended consequences' has to be deployed with skill, tact and persistence. Getting students to organize an inquiry is, in fact, an excellent way of giving them experience of the language of participation.

The second point, that the boundary between inquiry and participa-tion cannot always be neatly drawn, is illustrated by the Counthill techno-logy survey. In this project the school curriculum, a topic normally reserved for teachers' professional discourse, was addressed by the students, who persuaded staff to talk frankly about it and fed their findings back to them. For Counthill students to go round the school, with the teachers' sanction, asking curricular questions, was in itself a form of enhanced participation in the institution, rather than simply inquiry about it. The issuing of the report then took participation a stage further, in that the students now introduced their own meanings into a situation they had previously just asked about. Although confining themselves to reports of findings and impressions, and refraining (out of tact, at their teachers' suggestion) from offering recommendations, an alertness and sharpness in the writing reflected the students' awareness that their text, while not expressly designed to affect action, would be attentively read by those with the power to act.

Inquiry as a mode of engagement with the world cannot, therefore, be neatly contrasted with participation, as if the one simply represents the situation while the other seeks to change it. Both the design and the reporting of an inquiry can be charged with significance for potential action. Imparting researched information in the right way at a critical juncture can, indeed, change the situation.

If inquiry can be a mode of participation, so may participation display features we associate with inquiry. The language which students used within the overall purpose of trying to get something did not consist exclusively or even mainly of performatives. Urging, requesting, advising, warning, browbeating, reassuring, supporting and so on, with intent to affect the views and actions of co-actors, were only part of the business. Another part, more or less prominent in different situations, was reflection. In order to reach decisions about what to do, the students needed to generate the possibilities and reflect on them. In this process speakers were working less on each other than on their own representations as they sought to grasp and contemplate the realities and potential realities of their situation, including the likely effects and implications of this or that action, the relevance of particular previous experiences, whether the operation envisaged would be easy or difficult, fun or a drag, and the weight to accord to this or that consideration. In its truth-seeking aspect this phase of the participative mode has much in common with inquiry.

When we consider the typical outcome of a successful planning session – a sketch, orally realized, but often supported by written and graphical representations such as lists and flow-charts, representing a pattern of future actions and circumstances – we see that what the students are doing is designing. Design is at the centre of Donald Schön's *The Reflective Practitioner* (1983), a book which educators have seized on for its implications for teaching, but which can also throw light on what students do in 'situations of practice' (Schön's term). Reflection, says Schön, is central to effective action in 'messy' situations for which existing definitions, rules and precedents provide little guidance. Reflection comes into design (and other planning) at the point when a possible move has been tentatively delineated, bringing in its train all sorts of implications and potential consequences of which some are obvious, but others appear only under study. Reflection, then, is listening to this 'talkback' from the design so far realized.

In the DEFT projects, a clear relationship could sometimes be discerned between the effectiveness of students' action and the quality of their deliberation. The latter, in turn, was clearly language-linked. This observation enables us to make the connection between helping students use language as participants and English teachers' more typical concerns with the adequacy of students' representations and their imaginings of alternative experience.

4

Encouraging positive attitudes to language and learning among multilingual/bilingual speakers in schools: principles and practice

BERNARD T. HARRISON

The issues

> The world is like a mask dancing. If you want to see it well you do not stand in
> one place.   (Chinua Achebe, 1988: 365)

Some issues in education may grow from modest, even despised beginnings to act as a powerful nucleus for studies in learning and teaching. Examples such as a post-Piagetian concern for the importance of play in learning or gender issues in promoting equal educational opportunity might come to mind. Bilingual and multilingual issues have emerged as a further compelling instance, providing a focus for study of the education of ethnic or cultural minorities; of relationships between language, learning and culture; of educational disadvantage (including the increasing disadvantage that may be suffered by learners who have only monolingual competence in linguistically pluralist communities).

This paper aims to address, in particular, the overriding need of multilingual learners to learn. To be provocative (and to oversimplify), this takes

Acknowledgements Thanks are due to the following, who worked as members of the enquiry team: Janet Collins, Sandra Gittleson, Ian Jarvis, Chris Noble, Bernadette Walsh. All involved are grateful to the Educational Research Centre of the Division of Education, University of Sheffield and to Rotherham LEA for its financial support, and especially to those who generously gave their time and hospitality to the enquiry.

precedence even over issues of language or of culture, on which much has been written in recent decades. Learning can only take place, of course, through language and within culture, and the decades-long emphasis on them has not been misplaced. However, community-conscious educational policies will recognize that the actual clients of schools – the learners and their parents – look for an emphasis on what is taught and what learned. Many must be interested in the how, as well – but only as long as this also is concerned with issues of effective learning. Not surprisingly, this is a world-wide phenomenon, which may be compared to the universal expectation of all medical patients that they should be effectively treated or of all plain-tiffs in law that their cases should be effectively put. From a learner's (or parent's) point of view, education should provide preparation for and open-ings to the world that the learner expects to inherit. In the case of a child who has newly arrived with her parents from a rural Pakistani village into, say, Rotherham, her education should aim to equip her to take a place in an advanced industrial community – albeit in a setting that may show, at present, more signs of old industrial decay than of new development.

The phenomenon of multilingualism will come as a surprise only to the most insulated of the world's communities. It is generally accepted that there are about thirty times as many languages as there are countries in the world. Since most of the world's speech communities are then, multilingual, multi-lingualism is the norm, not the exception in language use. Britain is itself a clear example of a multilingual society (despite resistance to that fact among its monolingual groups, even in the face of impending full entry into Europe) and about half of the world population is bilingual (Grosjean, 1982).

To see multilingualism as 'a problem which affects the majority of the world's population' (Mackey, 1967) is to imply some kind of disability among multilingual/bilingual speakers, rather than to state a simple fact. Yet the literature on multilingualism and learning has, until quite recently, been dominated by attitudes that multilingual learners are linguistically – even intellectually – disadvantaged (Isaacs, 1976; Dorian, 1978; Sondergaard, 1981; Saunders, 1982). While there is no doubt that many multi/bilingual communities do, indeed, meet a number of social (including educational) disadvantages, more positive attitudes have now emerged to the global phenomenon of multi/bilingualism. Such readings as Benton (1985), Cummins and Swain (1986), Hakuta (1986), Moorfield (1987) and Romaine (1989) would support the view that 'from the conception of the bilingual as someone whose speech shows interferences and who is at worst cognitively deficient and at best the sum of two monolinguals, we have moved to the conception of an integrated person . . . for whom bilingual experience may enhance cognitive functioning' (Hamers and Blanc, 1989: 257). Multi/bilingualism may be seen, then, not only as a norm, but also as providing access to enhanced powers of communication; the 'problem', if any, is re-stricted to exclusively monolingual groups. 'Bilingualism at the societal

level will no longer be viewed as a stigma, but as a resource worth developing, since it can produce individuals with a unique set of languages,
cultures and experiences . . . of value to a multicultural world' (Hamers and
Blanc, 1989: 258).

Are all languages 'equal'?

This question contains, of course, a high political charge which requires
careful handling when policies are debated on multi/bilingualism in learning.
The attitudes of planners and teachers can sometimes be in danger of
polarizing, with one pole losing sight of the other. At one pole, the sheer
unfairness of cultural or linguistic hegemony in many multilingual contexts
is faced: 'Usually the more powerful groups in any society are able to force
their language upon the less powerful . . . In Britain, the British child does
not have to learn Panjabi or Welsh, but both these groups are expected to
learn English' (Romaine, 1989: 23). Efforts to recognize the equal claims of
all languages have resulted in 'immersion' programmes (such as total immersion courses in French for English-speaking Canadians) or in 'community'
language programmes (such as those developed in Australia in the past
decade or so).

At another pole are clustered powerful arguments – advanced not least
among many minority groups themselves – for ensuring that learners should,
above all, be fluent in the dominant national language, so that they may
claim their full share in the commercial, industrial, professional and political
life of the nation. Clearly, both of these poles provide essential guiding
principles for language policies in learning. There must be unqualified
respect shown for the cultural and linguistic identity of the learner, of whatever background; but the unquestioned rights of all learners to gain full
access to the power of the community must be fully protected – and since
language and society cannot be separated, this means that full access to the
dominant language must be part of that social process.

The dilemma presented by these poles is faced by Kalantzis *et al.* (1989),
who criticize what they see as educationally unsound aspects of the Australian Community Language Programme. They reject what they term the
'fruit bowl' version of simple pluralism which would offer to make no
distinction between one variety of language and another, and claim that 'we
are not duty-bound to conserve ancestral characteristics which are not struc-
turally useful. We are both socially determined and creators of human
futures . . .' (p. 18). In place of simple pluralism they offer a 'holistic' theory
of culture – 'the dynamic relationship of different levels of cultural activity'.
Their holistic model of culture in migration proposes three levels. Level 1
embraces all that is common, in the very nature of culture, to all human
cultures. Level 2 covers the major types of political-social-economic-cultural
customs to be found in human groups – including, for example, hunting and

gathering, peasantry, Western industrialization ('At this level First World societies today only have one culture: Western industrialism'). Level 3 is nearest to the 'fruit bowl' version of cultural diversity, including such differences in custom and behaviour as are to be found in varieties of food, dance, languages and celebrations. As Kalantzis *et al.* acknowledge, there are no deep reasons why levels 1 and 3 should cause serious problems in the process of multicultural assimilation. Level 2, however, contains all the potential seeds of real intercultural conflict.

A holistic-dynamic multicultural approach needs sensitive handling, in order to 'build pragmatically on existing traditions and cultures', but the principle of social equity should override pleas for linguistic pluralism at any cost. The robust stance taken by Kalantzis *et al.* may seem unkind, when applied to individual groups whose language and/or culture are at risk from a dominant language or culture; but their viewpoint carries undoubted force where decisions are being made about targeting limited educational resources on behalf of minority groups. Their concern, on behalf of learners in such groups, for access and equity has been adopted as a guiding principle for the study on which this paper is based. Alongside this, however, is a second guiding principle, that the original cultural and linguistic identity of individual learners and individual communities must be given unqualified respect, for that is where learners actually are, when the process of education begins in a new multicultural context.

The study

Multi/bilingualism is not a phenomenon of language as such, but of its use. The study of multi/bilingualism is sociolinguistic, investigating ways in which variant languages are used, and social attitudes towards them. Until recently, however, studies of usage have tended to concentrate on formal linguistic, rather than social aspects of multi/bilingualism. As for attitude studies, 'much less attention has been paid to the studying of attitudes towards bilingualism than other aspects' (Romaine, 1989: 7). In order to challenge traditionally negative or even hostile attitudes to multi/bilingualism in school education, and noting Romaine's own work on attitudes (with Asian parents now settled in Britain), it was decided to investigate enhanced attitudes in the policy and practice of educating multi/bilingual learners, mainly in primary/middle schools. Six local education authorities were chosen in the Midlands and North of England, all of which had well established language and multicultural policies. Four of these authorities had sizeable ethnically diverse school populations, while two had rather smaller (though steadily increasing) ethnically mixed groups in their schools. A language adviser was contacted in each authority, for advice on which schools might be approached in that authority in order to carry out the enquiry;

advisers were also interviewed on local education authority (LEA) and their own policies, practice and attitudes in this field.

The enquiry was conducted in two phases. In the first, advisers were individually interviewed and asked to nominate primary or middle schools where they felt that enhanced attitudes to the teaching of pupils with multi/ bilingual backgrounds had resulted in good patterns of language and learning. Each of these schools was then visited by one of the investigating team, where interviews were conducted with a teacher nominated by the adviser or headteacher (in some cases a teaching headteacher was the nominee), and with two pupils interviewed together, who were chosen by the headteacher or teacher. (All the pupils interviewed were of Asian background.) The school visits also included extended consultation with other staff, informal talks with other pupils in the school and classroom observation, as well as an examination of school resources. In the second phase of the enquiry, two of the LEAs were selected for further visits. In each of these, further schools were chosen for visits – mainly primary, but also secondary. Again, a nominated teacher and two pupils in each school were interviewed in a programme involving consultations and observation.

During their regular meetings throughout the enquiry the investigators reported on the whole notably welcoming responses from the advisers and schools. In only one authority was there any reluctance to be open about issues raised by the enquiry, although this was not through lack of enthusiasm for intentions. The advisers' difficulties were, rather, to do with their working in a politically sensitive climate, where it was thought unwise to allow direct recordings and transcriptions of their candid views on the issues raised, even though the usual full assurances had been given about anonymity of the research contexts and findings. The investigator found similar patterns in the school visits in this authority. He was made welcome, but had the experience of 'being what I imagine a client of Intourist might feel like. There was an air of idealism, but my intrusion was carefully circumscribed . . . It was suggested that I would not be successful interviewing the children and I was given a member of staff to help me' (Investigator's notes). Rather than expressing surprise at the experience of one investigator, the team as a whole agreed that reception of the enquiry, at LEA and school levels, had been unexpectedly candid, given that this can be an acutely sensitive area for enquiry.

The advisers

Semi-structured interview schedules with advisers were drawn up to cover a range of topics concerning attitudes to multi/bilingualism in schools. Information was sought on the number and proportion of multi/bilingual pupils and teachers in each LEA; about the main languages and overall number of languages used by school learners; and about the particular responsibilities that the adviser(s) carried for enhanced linguistic support in the LEA. Interviews moved on to explore such issues as linguistic 'difference' versus 'deficiency', the possible disadvantages of being monolingual, and attitudes to such terms as linguistic diversity and linguistic interaction. Comment was invited about the influence on the LEA concerned of the Bullock (DES, 1975) and Swann (DES, 1985) Reports, both of which had argued for linguistic support across the curriculum and against separate provision of support (which Swann condemned as 'institutional racism'); problematic aspects of integrated support were also explored. We then examined attitudes to proposals from the National Curriculum Council, especially the declaration in *English 5–16* (DES, 1989) that multi/bilingual children 'need to gain access to standard forms of English' (Chapter 10, 10.13). Comment was invited on the charge that this emphasis on Standard English reveals an unacceptable level of monolinguistic bias whereas 'The Cox Report' (DES, 1988a) placed more emphasis on linguistic diversity. Concerning policies and practice within the LEA, information was sought about the deployment of resources for linguistic support for multi/bilingual learners, on staffing/recruitment policies and on in-service provision to develop teachers' expertise in this area. Views were invited on the quality as well as range of such provision and how this might be enhanced. Finally, information and views were sought on LEA policies concerning mother tongue education, if any, for multi/bilingual pupils. Were there separate programmes for talking, listening, reading, writing? How much linguistic interchange was encouraged (for example, the use of Hindu terms in cross-cultural enquiries)? Were there policies on how parents might be contacted and brought into the life of the school? Was the LEA satisfied that its policies were genuinely and fully multicultural?

Now that LEAs are required to monitor numbers of multi/bilingual teachers and pupils, advisers are able to draw on easily available statistics. In four of the LEAs the number of multi/bilingual school pupils was in excess of 25 per cent and rising, while in the other two LEAs the proportion was less than 10 per cent. These figures represented more than seventy languages throughout the six LEAs, although the most common languages (about 80 per cent) were Punjabi and Urdu. Advisers acknowledged that problems arose because the overwhelming majority of their teaching forces were white and monolingual, and lacked training in the particular needs of the multi/bilingual pupils in their classrooms. The proportion of multi/bilingual teachers to the teaching population as a whole ranged from 2 to 4.4 per cent in these LEAs. Despite the efforts of advisers to secure qualified teacher status, where possible, for 'Section II' teachers, these figures remain worryingly slight. (Section II teachers are funded by the Home Office in Britain and are usually recruited from minority groups. They receive training towards qualifying as teachers while working as teachers in schools.)

As for attitudes to multi/bilingualism, there was solid agreement among

the advisers that, whatever problems faced them or their LEAs in implementing enlightened language policies, there was no essential educational
'problem' about being bilingual. The political stance of advisers on the needs
of ethnic minority groups did, however, show interesting differences. They
ranged from **radical-reforming**:

> The problem is not one of language as such but of race and colour . . . Schools
> must validate the experiences of their black pupils, but on the whole this is not
> happening,

to **moderate**:

> As long as bilingualism is perceived as a problem by staff in schools, it is a
> problem for the bilingual pupil – in the same way that racism is a problem for
> her, even though she herself is not possessed by racist attitudes,

to **cautious**:

> The idea, that a child with more than one language is in some way handicapped
> and has fluency in neither, I don't think is true.

This range of views was reflected in the range of LEA policies. In the
radical-reforming case, there was strong emphasis on the need to protect
the rights of pupils to use and develop their mother tongue, and the LEA's
Curriculum Statement on the need for mother tongue teaching of multi/
bilinguals was recognized and widely accepted in the schools. There was an
'excellent' programme for national examinations in community languages,
mainly Urdu, and the adviser felt that policies reflected the principle that
children in ethnic communities should be encouraged to remain bilingual –
'This should not be seen as an extra but as a necessity.'

In the **moderate** case, the adviser placed more emphasis on linguistic
diversity and interaction, in order to:

> encourage a positive attitude towards the multiplicity of languages that are
> spoken, not just in this country but across the world . . . By linguistic interac-
> tion, I mean we are encouraging schools to use the language within the school
> so that children share their languages and use them together.

He declared that he would be unworried about the 'intertwining' of languages within, say, a given Geography or History lesson and felt that this
should be welcomed as good practice, since children have concepts and skills
that they may not yet display adequately within their second language, but
would be able to achieve when encouraged to put their first language to the
service of working out a new idea or claiming a new piece of knowledge for
themselves.

In the **cautious** case, the adviser outlined what she called a 'transition'
policy, that was 'really a way of helping children adjust to an education
system that uses English as its medium; it is not seen as a way of promoting
bilingualism in the long term . . . ' She went on to describe support policies

which aimed to fulfil the recommendations of the Swann Report, which emphasized the need for integrated support in the teaching of English. This adviser disclosed that she still faced problems with schools which continued to operate 'withdrawal' policies in second language teaching, against the advice of the advisory service. 'We can quote Swann, we can quote HMI [Her Majesty's Inspectors of Education], but unless eventually the Home Office in its management of Section II and the rules it adopts, outlaws withdrawal approaches, there is little we can do to force change.' While this interviewee had little to say about protecting or encouraging the use of the mother tongue, she had interesting points to make about the issue of standard and other forms of English. Commenting on national curriculum proposals for English and the claim that bilingual children need to gain access to standard forms of English, she saw 'nothing problematic about that'; but she stressed that pupils should be able to operate 'competently and comfortably' in the language of their new community – which may be a variant, but not a lesser form of standard English – 'I am glad that the Cox Report has been very positive about accent and dialect.'

The interviews with advisers revealed, then, the tensions described in the first part of this paper, between the need to maintain an unqualified respect for the cultural and linguistic identity of learners, of whatever background, and their need for full access and equity in claiming possession of the dominant language of their new community.

The teachers

Of the ten teachers interviewed, eight were in primary schools and two were secondary teachers (in the second phase of the enquiry). Interview questions on background information and attitudes to bi/multilingualism covered similar ground to those put to advisers, but most of the interview time was used for exploring particular school qualities and classroom approaches with multi/bilingual groups. Questions were asked about the resources available to the school for linguistic support of these groups; about staffing/recruitment policies in this area, and about levels and quality of in-service provision for teacher development within the school and from the LEA. Turning to the classroom, how were multi/bilingual class groupings arranged? What approaches were practised to develop talking; reading; writing; paralingual activities, such as drama? How did teachers judge the 'climate' and quality of pupil–pupil and teacher–pupil relationships in their classroom and around the school? Interviewees were also asked about school policies on mother tongue teaching for bilinguals – the kinds of work done in the different areas of language work; whether language interchange was encouraged; how parents were contacted and brought into the life of the school; and whether, in their view, the school was 'genuinely multicultural' in its policies.

Predictably, the teacher interviews tended to show rather less concern with broad policy issues than with the actual language and learning approaches of their own school and classroom. However, comment on national and LEA policies was often given with a 'grass roots' forthrightness which was lacking in the interviews at adviser level. One teacher, for example, pointed out with a fine anger that he had been initially glad to support the LEA policy of closing down special reception centres for newly arrived ethnic minority children, so that they might go straight into mainstream education:

> When the centres closed we were actually promised that a vast improvement would go into bilingual classroom systems . . . We were all in favour of the centres closing at that time, assuming that there would then be provision within schools. Unfortunately, that was the first thing that ended up being cut. Not just in the area of bilingualism either. We have one child who is physically disabled, who needs a wheelchair sometimes – wears irons and so on – and to actually get support for that kind of special need is very difficult.

Another teacher acknowledged the excellent work done by her Authority in establishing a successful Ethnic Minority Support Service (including Section II teachers), but dwelled on the untidiness of operations at school level:

> We've had a series of meetings, just going through the different areas, trying to prepare record sheets starting from reception. Just trying to ensure progress, continuity . . . but it is a mammoth task.

Commenting as an employee of the financially poorest LEA that was visited, a third teacher admitted even to feeling guilty about the modest extra resources with which they had been provided – such as jigsaws, games, basic sorting materials and reading materials – because a neighbouring junior school without ESL children was desperately short of such materials for their pupils. 'I think we have spent a lot but possibly to the detriment of another area.'

All the teachers were impressed with their enlightened, strenuous concern to combat racism and to develop the best relationships possible within the ethnic groups in their care. Examples of practical action taken included insisting on mixed groups for football, visiting local mosques, linking with an Asian women's community group, never letting a racial insult pass without action being taken, establishing a bilingual radio station in the school (run by a teacher and technician, with pupils as presenters), and displaying welcoming and informative notices around the school in all the languages used by the pupils. In pressing her view that no culture or religion should ever oppress another, one teacher admitted her own reservations about requirements to include Christian teaching in the curriculum:

> I'm an atheist and in that sense I'm an outsider too. I'm much happier at the level of being considerate, kind, caring and that sort of social, moral teaching.

I'm quite happy with that, but to actually think of having to do Bible stories and things like that – I draw back immediately. I'll see what happens when it is enforced.

A few of the teachers interviewed acknowledged that there were problems of racism among teachers and pupils of their own school, but most interviewees wanted to stress the positive steps taken within their school to combat this, even when they expressed pessimism about racism in the community at large.

As for attitudes to Standard English and approaches to classroom practice in language teaching, the teachers revealed a notably more pragmatic approach to the issue of whether 'either' competence in English should be achieved at all costs, or learning should go along with the grain of the original language and culture of pupils. One teacher typically emphasized that her teaching approach began with the recognition that a child needs a personal identity:

> Obviously the thing that the child knows about is about him or herself, so probably first years will be doing 'Myself' and the child will be talking about himself, herself, life at home, the community and the school . . . We always start with their actual dialect, first-hand experience, before we try to do any work on it.

There was, however, a greater readiness among some teachers to move from the mother tongue to the use of English as rapidly as possible, as long as the confidence of the learner could be retained. Yet there were reservations: one teacher, while acknowledging that there must be access as soon as possible to standard forms of English, also insisted that 'the bilingual process is a gradual one' and that National Curriculum assessments might well be harmful to the confidence of bilingual children. Some interviewees showed considerable interest in and understanding of language operations. 'Orally, both Standard and Non-Standard English have their own rules of syntax, they have grammatical structures, they have formal basic sentences in the same way.' They took exception to what they saw as an over-anxiety in the National Curriculum English documents to move towards Standard English. 'The National Curriculum document should be a language document, not an English document.' It was heartening to note that all the teacher interviewees were quite clear about the difference between innate intelligence and initial lack of expertise in English or another language. One teacher provided a fascinating account of a maths lesson on long multiplication, where the frustrations and difficulties met by bilingual pupils were encapsulated:

> One pupil, non-English speaking, but very good at maths, was making a quite simple error which he brought to me. With my limited Panjabi and his limited English, we still could not manage to sort out what he was doing wrong. I then had to look round the class and find (a) someone who could do long multiplication and (b) someone who could explain. We found somebody who could

do a bit of each and attack the problem, but then ran into the problem that while pupils learn a concept in one language they may not have it in another. The pupil we had chosen to explain did not know what 'multiply' or 'divide' was in Panjabi. He knew how to do it and knew thousands of words in Panjabi, but because he'd learned multiplication in English, he did not know how to explain it in Panjabi. We were stuck . . .

A much happier outcome was described by another teacher:

One day I had a skeleton in the classroom and was doing work on parts of the body with young children. They were teaching me the words in Panjabi while I was teaching in English, so that not only was this a fun way of doing it but we were giving their home language status. It was also making certain that when I said, 'Your lungs are here', they actually knew what lungs were. They were able to say their names in Panjabi and then everybody else would say 'Yes, that's right'.

One of the secondary school teachers interviewed spoke with compassion about the anxieties of pupils' parents, even when these made life uncomfortable for her. She had been made aware, over her years of teaching ethnic minority groups, that parents could be both fiercely proud of their own origins and communities, while also being 'adamant that their children should get fluency in standard English', and that 'the mother-tongue language should not be used at all in school'. To sum up these interviews with the teachers, there was impressive evidence of great concern, goodwill, hard work and willingness to consider new ideas and approaches – especially when resources were available to accompany these. The approaches of the teachers were indeed pragmatic, but also characterized by generosity and genuine interest in their pupils. While acknowledging the demands of both parents and learners for access to standard English, they also understood that the notion of 'a language held in common' should work both ways:

I'm trying desperately to learn some Urdu, and the response from the pupils is quite amazing. Even being able to say just a few words, their response is incredible. They are so – I hope this doesn't sound patronizing – but grateful, that you're actually bothering to learn their language. And suddenly, they begin to see their language as more important than they at first thought. The only trouble is, it takes a long time . . .

The pupils

Interviews with the twenty pupils (sixteen primary, four secondary) provided fascinating data about their background, languages and attitudes to language, attitudes to school and to learning, and their hopes and plans. Three main points were identified from these interviews as being of particular relevance to the present paper.

The first was the remarkable confidence of all the pupils interviewed, even of those who had only been in the country for a few months. While the interview schedules were designed to highlight their positive experiences, it still came as something of a surprise when all interviewees asserted that not only were they coping with at least two cultures, but they also found much enjoyment in doing so. Indeed, many of the pupils were well used to being employed as a teaching resource:

Interviewer: Do you use Gujrati in the classroom?
Amite: No, usually English.
Tina: I have to speak Gujrati to this girl, she came from India, right? She doesn't understand English very much so we have to tell her meanings of things in Gujrati . . .
Amite: Same as in my class, there's this girl, right? I think she doesn't understand a lot, she doesn't understand Maths and English and everything, she's poor at reading and everything so we have to tell her in Gujrati what the meaning is.

Clearly, these two pupils were skilled in the familiar teachers' devices of explaining, cajoling and even putting uncomfortable pressure on their peers. The sturdy self-assertion of these pupils, all of whom spoke Gujrati or Panjabi, often belied the predictions of their teachers that they might be shy in interview. Some teachers insisted on being present during the interviews and these contained less flow of pupil talk. In one school the teacher insisted on conducting the interview himself, with the result that the transcript contained four-fifths of teacher dialogue, with mainly monosyllabic interjections from pupils. Given the space to express themselves, the pupils provided vivid accounts of their hopes and expectations – to travel widely, to be doctors, teachers, policewomen, journalists. One little girl aged 7, newly arrived from a rural village in Pakistan some five months previously, was asked where she would most like to live and answered without hesitation, 'Where I am. I like it here.'

A second interesting point was their handling of multilingual experiences. While all were adamant that English was the language of school and were agreed that it should be so, the pupils provided many vivid descriptions of the richly varied language contexts that they shared:

My dad, he's alright at English and his Gujrati is brilliant, and sometimes he speaks Panjabi because he's got a Panjabi friend who cannot speak English, so he talks to him and translates to him in English and things like that for other people; and my mum, she can speak Gujrati, her English is alright and she can also speak Hindi, because we've got a Hindi friend. My brother, he's only 6 years old and he can't speak very good Gujrati yet, he will be just joining the Gujrati school next year . . .

Other pupils explained in fascinating detail how and why they used a particular language at particular times in their lives. The comments of the pupils on their multilingual activities were characterized by zest, curiosity and confidence in handling language. This group of pupils showed far more language awareness than would be likely in any group of monolingual children, however bright and accomplished they might be.

A third notable feature of the pupil interviews was their high degree of interest in their school and education. Their interest was by no means conforming or uncritically approving; indeed, there were many vigorous recommendations made on how their school might be improved. One pupil, for example, complained with unexpected bitterness – among many approving remarks about his school and his teachers – about what he saw as the disgraceful state of the music room, particularly the disrepair of the equipment, including a guitar that he would clearly like to have played. Teachers were spoken of with approval, on the whole, and some with considerable affection; but teachers who 'shouted' and who were 'too strict about being tidy' were, predictably, not liked. One more, the sheer energy and curiosity of these children spilled out in their comments on schools and learning; all declared that they loved school outings and provided graphic, detailed accounts of them.

> We go to this manor in the country and stay there for two nights, and do things like tree trails. We look for certain trees with the map we've been given; we have to go to the places that are marked and find out what type of tree it is. Then we draw it. There is a photo trail, we are given a photo and we have to go to all the places that are marked on the map. You have to find out where it is and where the photo was taken. There was this Ice House right near the end of the fields. Me and my friend thought it would be a greenhouse made out of ice; instead it was just like a mound of earth with bricks that were put up like that in an arch shape. They put ice in there and meat to keep it cold.

These interviews cannot be easily summed up. What did emerge, overall, was that their strong sense of rootedness and belonging to their families was accompanied by an equally strong drive to discover, even to ransack their adopted community, and to make a successful conquest of it.

Summing up

The interviewers recognized that their selection of LEAs, teachers and pupils, and their handling of interview schedules were directed to highlight positive aspects of the experiences of learners as language users. The enquiry team recognized, of course, the considerable and important body of work that has shown a quite different picture of the experiences of ethnic minority children and which has exposed their vulnerability to apathy, prejudice, disadvantage and failure (see, for example, Cummins, 1984; Wells, 1987; Singh, 1988; Romaine, 1989). The team also acknowledges the considerable discrepancies and gaps between principles and practice that can exist at LEA level (see Singh's case studies of LEAs, 1988) and at teacher–pupil level in the handling of mother tongue languages (Cummins, 1984). What has emerged from **this** study is a view that positive attitudes to language and learning among multi/bilingual speakers are best achieved in LEAs and in schools where policies seek to go with the grain of the learner's own drive to learn, to inherit her/his community 'culture', and to establish an undisputed claim for a future in the community that we call Britain. If policies are unequivocally based on the perceived needs of learners, there should be less unhelpful polarized debate in the future about the rival claims of 'either' the rights of mother tongue speakers or the requirement to learn Standard English.

5 Critical language awareness and People's English

HILARY JANKS

People's English was part of a broad attempt on the part of the National Education Crisis Committee to establish People's Education for People's Power in South Africa during the late 1980s (see Janks, 1990). The draft proposals for People's English maintained that if the study of English is to empower students and serve as a vehicle for liberation, language competence must include the ability:

to say and write what one means
to hear what is said and what is hidden
to defend one's point of view, to argue, to persuade, to negotiate
to create, to reflect, to invent
to explore relationships, personal, structural, political
to speak, read and write with confidence
to make one's voice heard
to read print and resist it where necessary
to understand the relationship between language and power.
                    (National Education Crisis Committee, Press Release, 1986)

Henrietta Dombey (1987) advocated a similar aim for English teaching in Britain:

The teaching of English is powerful stuff . . . It's hardly surprising that teachers of English are an irritant to the government . . . We are clearly not in the business of teaching our pupils to be obedient workers, docile citizens, and eager consumers. Instead we are primarily concerned with putting our pupils in charge of their own lives. Learning to be sensitive to the ways others use language, which means in part to recognize manipulation, deception and coercion, protects our pupils from exploitation.

The South African government was certainly 'irritated' by People's Education; irritated enough to ban the National Education Crisis Committee in 1987, to detain without trial the members of its executive and to declare discussions relating to People's Education prohibited under a state of emergency and subject to vast punitive action by the state.

This was prior to 2 February 1990, when President F.W. de Klerk announced sweeping reforms for South Africa. At the end of February 1991 a joint working group on education, made up of anti-apartheid educationists and government representatives, was established by the State at the request of a delegation led by Nelson Mandela. The brief of the working group was to define 'procedures to establish a full representative forum to discuss a new education system' (*Weekly Mail*, 1 March 1991: 5). Its supporters hope that a new education system in a democratic South Africa will encourage critical thinking instead of outlawing it.

It is to this end that I have begun to write and research Critical Language Awareness materials for secondary schools. Where syllabuses, examinations and teacher education are largely under the control of the State, the only pro-active gap that exists under the present system is to develop alternative materials. 'Alternative' has come to mean counter-hegemonic in South African discourse. In addition, a new education system is going to need such materials. Materials development can constitute a top-down intervention which is *not* empowering for the teacher, but without the existence of alternative materials it is difficult to educate teachers to produce their own. Creating them is a first step.

Since 1976, the date of the Soweto uprising, teachers in black education have been seriously disempowered. At the interface between the Department of Education and Training (DET – the State education department responsible for implementing Bantu Education policies) and the students, it is teachers who have borne the brunt of the student revolution. Under-prepared by DET schools and training colleges, teaching apartheid syllabuses which allow them no voice, using English, a language in which they are not always confidently fluent, teachers have struggled to maintain the respect of their students. One of the main aims of the newly formed South African Democratic Teachers' Union (SADTU) is to re-establish the position of the teacher as someone from whom students can learn. Providing teachers with classroom materials that take People's English seriously may contribute to this process.

In an attempt to redress the top-down nature of a materials intervention, I have been developing the materials module by module, in four stages, using action research. (I have used an action research spiral whereby successive modules are developed on the basis of what is learnt from the process of writing and researching earlier modules.)

Stage 1
I write a first draft of the module.

Stage 2
I select schools in which to do my primary research and bring the teachers who will teach the materials in the schools into the materials development research team. In redrafting the materials, I attempt to reconcile the needs of all the teachers from the different schools.

For Module I, I used a non-racial independent school and an independent black school. At the time, state schools were too tightly controlled for politically sensitive materials to be researched, though this may no longer be the case.

Stage 3
The students are brought into the research team prior to their teachers teaching them from the materials. I explain my research to them and tell them that their responses to the materials will be used in two ways:
1 Their responses inform the final re-drafting of the materials for publication.
2 They inform the drafting of the next module.

The form in which their responses are given (interviews, questionnaires, notes written onto copies of the module) is negotiated with the students.

During Stage 3 the teachers and the students use the module in the class-room. In addition to the materials being used in these schools selected for my primary research, other schools are simultaneously trialling the materials. This provides an additional or secondary source of feedback on the materials gathered by questionnaires.

Stage 4
I collate the primary and secondary responses to the module from both students and teachers. Where the suggestions for redrafting the materials differ, the teachers and students in the primary research group help me to make final editing decisions. That module is published, and then Stage 1 of the next module begins.

This process is empowering for all the students and teachers who are involved in the development of the materials. For them the materials are not imposed. Once the materials have been published for use by other teachers and students, this is, of course, no longer true. In an attempt to mitigate this imposition, each module encourages students to reflect on the module itself using the Critical Language Awareness skills that the module teaches. This is made explicit in the Foreword to the module which is addressed to the students:

> I am hoping that your growing language awareness will enable you to read crit-ically. What I mean by this is that when you read and listen you will be ready and able to challenge what writers and speakers say and how they say it. It. You will oppose what you read and hear before deciding to accept it; in other words you will learn to become oppositional readers.
>
> I hope that this will also make you ready and able to challenge what I say and the way I say it too. After all I am just another writer. Every workbook in the series includes an exercise at the end which asks you to question and even to resist what the workbook is doing to your thinking. I suggest that you keep this in mind from the first exercise.   (Janks, in press)

Before turning to a discussion of Module I, I need to provide a rationale for the selection of Critical Language Awareness (CLA) as the focus for my materials. The work of the Language-Ideology-Power research group at Lancaster University (Clark *et al.*, 1987) and my own research (Janks, 1988) argues the need for a 'critical' dimension to language study. Critical Language Study (CLS):

> ... is a resource for developing the consciousness and self-consciousness of dominated people ...
> ... their linguistic consciousness, that is, of how their familiar social practices are shaped, in their linguistic dimensions, by exploitative relations of power. The assumption is that consciousness is a necessary, though not sufficient, condition for social emancipation, and it is this assumption and commitment to emancipation which underlie the notion of making Language Awareness critical.   (Clark *et al.*, 1987: 27)

Part of the role of language in human life is to maintain and reproduce the existing social order. It is also in and through language that the existing social order is contested. Language is itself a site of struggle. Words do not have meanings of their own. They are put to use in conflicting discourses so that the sign is a battleground of opposing meanings. Language is not an innocent medium. Critical Language Awareness (CLA), which places language study in the context of power relationships, can provide students with the means to see through the positions and intentions which shape the linguistic forms. In addition, it should help them to understand how the linguistic forms are themselves used to shape perceptions.

Dissimulation, legitimation and reification are the three interrelated processes by means of which language sustains and reproduces relationships of domination (Thompson, 1984: 131). CLS aims to enable students to question common-sense assumptions and conventions which give legitimacy to dominant values; it aims to enable them to deconstruct and denaturalize dominant discourse; it aims to enable them to 'hear what is said and what is hidden':

> Critical is used in the special sense of aiming to show connections which may be hidden from people, such as the connections between language, ideology and power ... CLS analyses social interactions in a way which focuses upon their linguistic elements, and which sets out to show their generally hidden determinants in the system of social relationships, as well as hidden effects they may have upon that system.   (Fairclough, 1989: 5)

The aims of both CLS and CLA match the political aims of the People's English proposal. These aims make explicit the political ideology which underpins People's Education and makes no attempt to pretend that education is ideologically neutral. People's English should enable learners:

> to understand the evils of apartheid and to think and speak in non-racist, and non-sexist and non-elitist ways;
> to determine their destinies and free themselves from oppression;
> to play a creative role in the achievement of a non-racial democratic South Africa;

to express and consider the issues and questions of their time;
to transform themselves into full and active members of their society.
(National Education Crisis Committee, 1986)

These aims have to be seen against the context of Bantu education which aimed to keep the 'native' in his place: 'there is no place for [the Bantu] in the European community above the level of certain forms of labour' (Verwoerd, 1954).

The aims of language competence with which I began should be seen, within the context of the draft proposal, as a means of achieving these political aims. The choice of CLA in South Africa is a political commitment to education for democracy.

Helping students 'to understand the relationship between language and power' is foregrounded as an aim of the materials in the Foreword which is addressed to students.

> *Language and Position* is the first workbook in a series. I have called the series *Language Matters* because I want to teach you that there is a relationship between language and power. There can be little doubt that power matters, both to people who have it and to those who do not. What these language materials do is raise your awareness about language so that you can come to understand the connections between language and power.
>
> *Language Matters* will try to raise your consciousness about how language helps people to gain power and how it helps to take power away from people. If it succeeds you should become more able to resist language that lessens your power.   (Janks, in press)

Language and Position attempts to work with concepts from critical theory such as 'ideology' (Althusser, 1970; Thompson, 1984) 'subject position' (Althusser, 1970), 'preferred reading' (Hall, 1980), 'naturalized conventions' (Clark *et al.*, 1987: 22), 'myth' (Barthes, 1973), the 'plurality of meaning' (Volosinov, 1973) and 'determinism versus agency' (Giroux, 1983) in such a way as to make them useful tools for oppositional reading. In most instances the concepts are not named, but students are given ways of manipulating them. The module builds student understanding of 'position' by working from physical and then geographical positioning through social and historical positioning to an integrated exploration of the contextual determinants of meaning.

'Where we stand affects what we "see"' (p. 1) and 'Where we stand matters' (p. 2) begin the module by discussing position literally. Where we are physically in space can affect our understanding of the thing we are trying to know such as an elephant or a two-coloured block. It can also affect our interpretation of an event such as a sports match, an accident or a riot. This results in more than one account of things and events: meaning is plural.

' "Up" is good, "down" is bad' (p. 3) starts to move away from the literal by asking students to consider the 'evaluative accents' (Volosinov, 1973: 80) of 'up' words and 'down' words in English. In *Metaphors We Live By*,

Lakoff and Johnson (1980) show that 'up' expressions in English (I'm on top of the world; we have high standards; that boosted my spirits) have positive evaluative accents whereas 'down' expressions have negative ones (I'm feeling down; he dropped dead; things are at an all time low).

'Up'/good and 'down'/bad expressions are then tied to conventional ways of representing the world in maps. Conventionally, maps show north as 'up' and south as 'down'. 'Where's the top?' (p. 4) and 'North is up and south is down but the world is round' use the globe as text and challenge conventional ways of representing the world. At the end of the module (p. 27) students are asked to analyse an alternative map of the world used in Australian and Japanese schools which places these two countries at the centre of the world with Africa and Europe in the West and America in the Far East. Clark *et al.* (1987: 22) see the denaturalization of conventions as one of the theoretical underpinnings of CLS. 'Who draws our maps? Whose interests are served by these drawings?' are important questions for a critical education. Although maps focus on semiotics removed from language, these pages ask students to talk and read in English and the linguistic encodings of living 'down under' or in the 'far east' are not forgotten. In addition, students are encouraged to use their CLA across the curriculum.

'Standpoint or point of view' (p. 6) and 'Positions based on who we are' (p. 7) move students to a metaphorical understanding of 'position'. People's subject positions on political, emotional and intellectual issues are likely to be affected by who they are and what they believe. Students are given exercises which ask them to consider how gender, age, race and language loyalty might influence their attitudes. They are also asked to suggest other influencing factors and to consider to what extent people's subject positions are determined by their social circumstances and to what extent they can act as free agents. This is followed by a role-play exercise in 'How we use language to position other people' (p. 8). Two competing siblings have to use language in such a way as to win their mother over to their position.

Writers also use language to position their readers. Students are asked to consider four texts by four different writers: a poet, an advertiser and two historians writing about the same battle (pp. 9–12). The questions on each text facilitate oppositional reading. These questions are typical:

1 How does 'I' present herself/himself in the first stanza? How do you feel about 'I' after reading stanza 1?
2 How does 'I' change position in stanza 2? Do you feel the same or different about 'I' after reading stanza 2?
3 What does this word tell us about the writer's attitude?
4 How does this word influence the reader?
5 Why is this information placed at this point in the passage?
6 How does the writer give the impression that God is on the side of the trekkers? Why is this important?

7 Imagine that you are an Ndebele warrior or woman from the tribe. Write your own version of what happened.
8 How do the two versions of the same battle differ? How do they compare with the version in *your* school's textbook?

'History from above and history from below' (p. 13) develops the issues raised by the two accounts of the historical battle. History from above is history told from the point of view/position of the conquerors. History from below is the same history told from a different point of view, from the point of view of the conquered or the underclasses. This revises a number of concepts already covered: the plurality of meaning, subject position and up/down language. Students are given Brecht's poem 'Questions of a worker reading history' and are asked to think of questions that a worker could ask of South African history.

'Noah's Ark: the story told from below' is an example of history from below. It offers an imaginative account of the old testament story told by those who drowned in the flood because they were forced to watch

> ... as Noah set to work. He had the tools, he had the knowledge. Where did he get the hammers? Where did he get the nails?
> (Junction Avenue Theatre Company, 1987)

Before leaving history, students are asked to think about naming practices: 'Names from history: whose history?' (p. 15). The introductory exercise asks students to compare street names in Rhodesia's Salisbury with street names in independent Zimbabwe's Harare. They are then asked to think about names in their own towns which they think should be changed and why. There is a further exercise on the naming of public holidays. South Africa's public holidays are strongly contested. Anti-apartheid organizations and most of black South Africa commemorate Sharpeville day (21 March) and Soweto day (16 June) by work stay-aways because they are not official public holidays. The 'black calendar' or the 'alternative calendar' affects the economy of the country as well as school and university calendars. May Day was another holiday on the alternative calendar. The State has finally included it as an 'official' public holiday, but has called it 'Workers' Day'. The State has also renamed its holy days in the hope that they will survive independence. For example, van Riebeeck Day is now Founders Day and Easter Monday has become Family Day. The name changing is tied to a political contest: students see language working in relation to social forces in general and to history in particular. This view of meaning as grounded in history and social struggle is derived from critical theory and is a lynch pin of CLA.

Meaning is tied to context: social, political, economic, historical. Positions are not free-floating: they are negotiated in discourse dialogically; in discourse which is itself 'a practice of struggle' (Clark *et al.*, 1987: 24):

Even the most primitive human utterance produced by the individual organism is, from the point of view of its content, import, and meaning, organised outside the organism in the extraorganismic conditions of the social milieu. Utterance as such is wholly a product of social interaction, both of the immediate sort as determined by the circumstances of the discourse, and of the general kind, as determined by the whole aggregate of conditions under which any given community of speakers operates.   (Volosinov, 1973: 93)

'How context helps to position readers' (p. 16) is, therefore, fundamental to this module on the relationship between language and position. In the first exercise on context a teacher says 'I'm sorry' to the principal of her school as an expression of sympathy and fellow feeling, but is understood to be apologizing. What the principal 'heard' introduced the notion that the teacher might be at fault. The teacher and the principal were not using 'sorry' in the same way. Tannen (1990), from whom the story is taken, attributes the different understandings of the word to gender. The fact that the principal is the teacher's boss is at least as material. Bosses expect their workers to apologize if something goes wrong. His position makes him more likely to 'hear' an apology. Had *he* said 'I'm sorry' the teacher would have been less likely to think her boss was apologizing for suspending the boy, as if suspending him was wrong. Students are asked to collect examples from their own experience to show that

> words change their position according to the position held by those who use them.   (Pecheux, 1975: 111)

Who is speaking or writing and who is listening or reading is part of the context of meaning.

When and where are also part of the context. A 1931 cigarette advertisement is used to discuss how 'When is part of the context'. In the decades since the advertisement was written, medicine has shown that cigarette smoking causes heart disease and lung cancer, rendering absurd claims such as 'Don't rasp your throat with harsh irritants, reach for a Lucky instead' and 'Luckies are always kind to your throat'. Readers no longer share the 'common sense' (Gramsci, 1971) of the 1930s. It is easy for them to resist the advertisement's interpellative hail (Althusser, 1970: 48).

In 'Where is part of the context?' students are asked to think about the different meanings of the word 'international' when it is used in different contexts. 'International' has a peculiarly South African meaning ever since it was applied to certain five-star hotels that were granted 'international' status in the 1970s. What this meant is that they were allowed to admit people of all races and, secondly, that they were allowed to serve them liquor! Because the word 'international' could signify 'foreign blacks', it was selected to account for the otherwise anomalous suspension of two of apartheid's sacred cows. However, this is not the end of the story. No sooner has one accustomed oneself to this meaning of the word, than it slips in a different context. In 1985 the Pretoria Zoo boasted 'international toilets'. Desegregated toilets in the heart of the laager one might think, until one sees *where* they are situated: right next to a block of toilets marked 'Toilette blankes Toilets whites'. The adjacent block complicates the decoding of the sign.

What we know is also part of the context. Two sequential advertisements are used to show students this. In 1990 Mercedes Benz won an international advertising award for this advert:

> The advertisement was based on a true story. A man was driving a Mercedes Benz on Chapman's Peak in Cape Town. Chapman's Peak is a very steep, curving road along the side of a mountain with the Atlantic ocean below. The car went over the cliff and crashed on the rocks below. Because the front and back of the Mercedes Benz are designed to concertina on impact leaving the passenger compartment intact, the driver was not hurt. The advertisement emphasises this safety feature.

In the same year BMW produced this advert:

> The BMW advertisement showed a BMW travelling down the same road as the Mercedes Benz. The BMW does not go over the cliff and the slogan for the advertisement is 'BMW beats the bends'.   (Janks, in press: 20)

Because the BMW advertisement is a response to the Mercedes advertisement, the Mercedes advertisement is the context which determines the meaning of the BMW advertisement. This introduces the students to the concept of intertextuality; to an understanding of how the relationships *between* texts affect meaning. This understanding is further developed in the next exercise in which students are asked to think about how pictures can affect our interpretation of written texts which they accompany. In 'Pictures are part of the context' students are asked to consider how different pictures and cartoons of Chief Mangosuthu Buthelezi position the 'reader' differently.

The last four pages of the module consist of five texts for students to read critically using what they have learnt in the module on position. There are two texts on black taxi drivers: same topic, different positions. There is an advertisement to protest the harvesting of seals, and the map of the world used in Australian and Japanese schools. The fifth text is explained to the students as follows

> The last text [for analysis] requires some explanation. It is this module on *Language and Position* that you have been working through. It is also a text. As I said in the *Foreword*, I am no more neutral than any other writer. I am also attempting to position you, my readers. This module is different from traditional language text books. How is it different? What are the effects on you of these differences?   (Janks, in press: 22)

They are also given questions to help them with their analyses. These questions serve as a reminder of issues raised in the module. Students are asked to think of other questions that would help them to 'oppose' and 'interrogate' the five texts. They are also asked to try using the questions on self-selected texts:

1 Before you read the texts you need to work out what your views are on the topics they discuss. How might these views affect the way you respond to and interpret the texts?

2 How is your response to the text affected by who you are?

3 What do you know about the readers for whom the text was written?

4 How are the writers using language to position the readers? Examine the words they have chosen to influence their readers. Explain their effects.

5 Who is the author? What organization/newspaper/institution does the author work for?

6 What do we know about each author's positions from what they have written?

7 How many points of view are given in the text? Which of these are given the most support by the writer? What points of view are missing?

8 How does the context help to position the reader?

9 How do pictures, layout and spacing help the writer to position the reader?

(Janks, in press)

Language and Position is the first module in a series specifically designed to teach students that language does matter. If it succeeds in educating students to read critically, it will have taught them something about the relationship between language and power, and their own ability to resist subjection. 'Resistance' is not a word used lightly in the South African context. It is resistance that has led to the collapsing of apartheid, a system of oppression which affects every aspect of daily life in South Africa. Students know how to resist coercion. Since 1976 they have been a significant part of a resistance movement that has challenged the powerful repressive apparatuses of the State. Domination is, however, not only maintained by coercion. What a critical education can do is empower students to resist the State's ideological machinery as well. *Language and Position* is a small contribution to that endeavour.

6 Literary literacy, censorship, and the politics of engagement

DEANNE BOGDAN

The meta-problem

In focusing on a rationale for literary literacy rather than a definition of it, I raise a meta-problem that brings together three main issues about literature in schools: the present place and function of the language arts curriculum, the increasing censorship of literary texts and the rise of the 'response model' in literary pedagogy. These issues are current manifestations of ongoing problems arising the formulation of the why, what, and how of literary education, problems that can be termed the problems of justification, censorship and response. These can be understood as components of a meta-problem because of their intrinsic connectedness: justice cannot be done to the analysis or to the resolution of any one of these if each is viewed in isolation. Today, educators' basic assumptions, implied in their formulation of the why, what and how of literary education, bear re-examination in terms of the overlapping nature of the three elements of this meta-problem. Specifically, I contend that rationales for the educational value of literature, as propounded in official guidelines for the subject, are on a collision course with rationales against censorship. That is, I see an inconsistency in the reasoning used to justify literature in the curriculum on the one hand, and typical rebuttals to censors on the other. I also claim that the pedagogical shift from literary analysis and the study of literary 'masterpieces' to the 'personal growth', 'reader response' and 'transactional' models (Moffett,

An earlier version of this paper was published as 'Toward a rationale for Literary Literacy' in *The Journal of Philosophy of Education*, Vol. 4, No. 2, 1990, pp. 211–224. The author is indebted to James Cunningham and Hilary Davis for their comments and suggestions for this revised version.

1968; Britton, 1970; Dixon, 1979; Rosenblatt, 1985; Dias, 1987; Bogdan and Straw, 1990), inasmuch as this shift reinforces changes in curriculum content, has vital implications for dealing with the justification and censorship of literature texts.

Plato first posed the meta-problem by banishing the poets from his Republic. Ever since, arguments against censorship and in support of the educational value of literature have had to counter his central claim: if literature can influence for good, it can also do so for ill. In the history of Anglo-American letters, every defender of literature as a vehicle for moral education has had to ask why and how the power of literary art is a good thing and not a bad one. From Sir Philip Sidney in the Renaissance, to Percy Bysshe Shelley and Matthew Arnold in the nineteenth century, to T.S. Eliot, F.R. Leavis and Northrop Frye in the twentieth, poets, scholars, and critics have taken up Plato's challenge; however, as I hope will become clear, perhaps they have not taken it seriously enough.

The 'why' of literature education: 'enculteration' and 'transformation'

Over the past decade or more, the traditional humanist belief in the educational value of literature as intrinsic and inviolate has been challenged by the shift in emphasis in literary criticism from the text to the reader (Fish, 1970, 1980; Bleich, 1978, 1986; Iser, 1978, 1980; Tompkins, 1980) as well as by the privileging of personal enjoyment, free response and 'engagement with the text' (Dixon, 1967, 1979; Rosenblatt, 1978, 1985) over literary appreciation of an accepted canon. These shifts are a departure from the rubric of the old 'poetics of detachment' which assumed as a given the enriching value of literary experience and concentrated instead on rooting out 'stock' and 'uneducated' responses in readers. Prior to these shifts, the humanist position was not particularly problematic, and literary literacy fulfilled a dual educational aim – 'enculteration' and 'transformation', compatible goals in a society that presumably intended the transmission of an existing cultural heritage through exposure to canonical texts.

In 1989 the Canadian pundit of literature and the arts, Robert Fulford, spoke about the presumed consonance between political enculteration and personal transformation in a lecture, 'Literature and Literacy: The Future of English Studies'. He addressed the 'central problem of education in our time' which he saw as 'the culture of illiteracy' (p. 8). He cited the philosophy of literature education propounded by George Paxton Young, 'a nineteenth-century . . . visionary' (p. 1) who was influential in infusing into the colonies a healthy dose of Arnoldian fervour about the power of literature to mould the moral lives of students. For Young, literature was to be the core of the curriculum because of its unique capacity for mental stimulation and character formation. Quoting Young, Fulford delivered a paean to literature education that championed the 'exquisite thoughts and images . . . [of Arnold's] sweetness and light . . .' (Fulford, 1989: 7).

Here the development of the moral-literary sensibility is seen to achieve both enculteration into a political and social ethos inherent in the great tradition of canonized writers, and the transformation of the individual psyche from ignorance of 'exquisite thoughts and images' to enlightenment and purification by them. This cultural ideal, Fulford argued, has persisted undisturbed from the last century into our own through the teachings of, among others, F.R. Leavis and Northrop Frye, who also believed in the capacity of the moral and the literary to predispose students to acuteness of feeling and mental receptivity.

Am I suggesting that this has now changed? Yes and no. Humanist claims about character formation were evident, for example, in the 1977 Ontario Guideline Curriculum (Ontario Ministry of Education, 1977), and this humanist espousal of the 'centrality of literature' to the curriculum remains in the 1987 version (p. 2). However, whereas in the earlier document there was a consonance between enculteration and transformation, in the later one there is something of a disjunction. A rhetorical analysis of the 1987 guideline document (see Bogdan, 1989) discloses a conflation of the two goals within a philosophy of literature education tacitly at odds with itself because of an unconscious ambivalence about the double-edged nature of literary power. Echoing the ideal of the moral-literary sensibility is an uncritical acceptance of the 'power' of literature which is presumed automatically to empower students to self-actualization; but now this empowerment, redolent of the humanist character of the moral-literary sensibility, must, it seems, be harnessed in support of quite specific cultural goals, such as nationalism, pluralism and feminism (p. 2).

As a feminist myself, I am not challenging these goals. Rather I want to stress that, whereas formerly literary literacy was regarded as the logical outcome of reading canonical texts, now it breaks down, on the one hand, into personal development and psychic change through engagement with the text and, on the other, into politically correct values that are to be inculcated through the judicious selection of textual content, such as Canadian literature, literature of minorities and literature about and by women. Yet the persistence of the humanist legacy, in which the 'right' values wrought by the moral-literary sensibility are deemed to emanate from the study of literature *sui generis*, blankets over the gap now existing between transformation and enculteration as the two related but discrete goals of literature education. A clash of world-views among professionals, students and parents is bound to occur when the double-edged 'power' of literature 'to shape thought and understanding' (Ontario Ministry of Education, 1987: 2) is being implemented by an ever-expanding and contracting syllabus of literary content and the pedagogy of 'the response model' (which takes seriously literary experience as 'real' experience), is being resisted by those who fear that the departure from the Arnoldian ideal will seduce their children away from traditional values.

To illustrate this tension between conflicting world-views, let us examine the trends towards the implementation of the 'reader response' principle as a given in literature education and the harnessing of literary experience in the service of social goals. In literary education today, course material has had to keep pace with calls for its social relevance (itself a problematic assumption) in an increasingly pluralistic society; and the 'response' model, premised on honouring the 'free' intuitive reactions of students (Dias, 1987), has replaced 'the pedagogy of detachment' (Bogdan and Yeomans, 1986). These trends have created a veritable spawning ground for censorship in the classroom, where one student's self-realization is bound, sooner or later, in a society as socially diverse as Canada's, to become another's self-alienation. This situation is rendered even more problematic by a governmental mandate to inculcate students through literature into culturally specific goals believed to be compatible with that of personal development, without provision for the anomalies that will inevitably ensue. Literature education aims simultaneously at social and cultural identity, and at a self-identity which may – and should – include social and cultural critique. These two goals are not mutually exclusive, but neither are they necessarily mutually reinforcing in today's classroom as they may have been when moral-literary sensibility by itself was thought to hold the key to both and when the poetics of detachment ensured that the 'uneducated' response would be held at bay.

At the heart of the meta-problem lies the subversive element in the psychodynamics of literary experience. Though all three issues of the meta-problem – the changing canon, the response model, and calls for censorship – presuppose the power of literary experience, the probability that its double-edged power often precipitates a journey into self-doubt and social conflict is eclipsed by naive belief in the dialectic of the educational process, which is presumed to reconcile all disparities. I do not say that it will not; but the educational process, as teachers know too well, never takes place in the abstract. The following case study will perhaps show how the enmeshment of the justification, censorship, and response problems is embedded in the day-to-day lives of teachers and students.

The 'what' of literature education: canon, curriculum, censorship

Two years ago the English Department of a Toronto secondary school with a large population of black students complied with a request from a black student movement to remove from the curriculum William Golding's *Lord of the Flies* (1954) because some students were offended by a single line which referred to blacks pejoratively. 'Which is better – to be a pack of painted niggers like you are, or to be sensible like Ralph is?' (p. 221). How could those members of the polarized English faculty who voted against the book have rationalized such a decision when their training in literary context and their commitment to literary values would normally have militated against judging the work racist? In trying to answer this question, I will deliberately heighten the tension between enculteration and transformation, selection and censorship, and engagement and detachment.

Enculteration and transformation are directly related to three givens of the literature curriculum: sympathetic identification, vicarious experience and social relevance. On the one hand, literature is supposed to lead into and out of the individual 'self' by way of a positive engagement with the text; on the other, it is expected to result in that self accommodating and assimilating the values of the society in which its future citizens are to dwell. It is not difficult to see how these two aims of self realization and enculteration are diametrically opposed in the above case of *Lord of the Flies*. These black students are being enculterated into an ethos of liberal humanism, which prizes racial tolerance and celebrates the multicultural fabric of Canadian national identity; but, as readers of *Lord of the Flies*, they are being asked to identify against themselves, that is, to participate in an experience that explicitly excludes them (Fetterly, 1978). The argument that the Golding novel is a 'classic' whose expulsion threatens cultural literacy conflicts with other criteria simultaneously operating in selecting curriculum, for example, ease of positive identification, a principle supported by English departments, upon which the adolescent fiction industry thrives. Defending *Lord of the Flies* as a classic harkens back to the discipline of English studies informed by the poetics of detachment and the 'humanizing' value of the canon. To honour positive identification in one context and dismiss it when it becomes inconvenient, to subordinate the ideals of cultural heritage and literary context in order to make the curriculum more socially relevant, but to advocate those ideals in response to the objections of one group of students, especially when the 'inconvenient' or objecting group is a minority in a culture whose diversity is otherwise touted as a mark of national identity, is at best anomalous and at worst racist. Within this context, enculteration and transformation seem not just incongruent, but counterfeit.

Educators cannot embrace an affirmative action curriculum policy that seeks to engender attitudinal change and then suddenly cry 'Censorship!' when that policy is interpreted by those students whom it purports to liberate as allowing them the right not to read books that, for them reinforce the very psychic anguish that affirmative action seeks to counteract. Again, I have no quarrel with the revisionist political objectives in the Ontario guideline document, but rather with current assumptions about how they are to be attained through the literature curriculum. The power of literary naming, the emotional force of literature, and the 'reflectionist' theory of literature as an imitation of life (Moi, 1985) are still largely regarded as unproblematic. The uncritical privileging of these notions can result in a curriculum policy which can all too easily apply with apparent impunity the double standard of accepting the criterion of positive identification in the case of young adult fiction, but of rejecting it in the case of the black students' deposition to remove *Lord of the Flies*. That the first instance constitutes the adding of material and the second the subtracting of it does not alter the unacknowledged bias in the decision; nor does it erase the power differential between the assumed rights of the dominant to transmit their culture and the 'obligation' of the marginalized to accept it in a society that boasts equality for all (see 'The Development of a Policy on Race and Ethnocultural Equity', Ontario Provincial Advisory Committee on Race Relations, 1987).

At the same time, there is the danger of so sanitizing the curriculum by trading off strong literature for pap that no student's interest would be engaged by it anyway, and of perpetuating in the name of sensitivity the very chauvinism toward women and minorities that a fair curriculum policy would attempt to eliminate. For, if literary works adjudged over centuries to be worthy of study are continually bypassed in the public school classroom, they become museum pieces to be known only by an elite, who through accident of social privilege, time and place, are privy to an esoteric cultural legacy, a legacy by which the majority of students, not included in the elite, will be judged uneducated.

The pluralist solution is to strike a balance among various literary pictures of the world. Here the problem is three-fold. Firstly, it gives equal weight to all points of view, thus undercutting the intent of affirmative action. Secondly, it turns on the reflectionist theory of literature challenged by much recent literary theory (Widdowson, 1982; Moi, 1985; Weedon, 1987). Thirdly, it perpetuates the conflation of enculteration and transformation as educational goals as in the expectation that a humanist pluralism will be a by-product of the 1990s version of moral literary sensibility. For example, in the 1987 Ontario document, the 'centrality' of literature to the curriculum is argued on the basis of its 'power' as a reflection of life, as 'an inspiring *record* of what men and women have enjoyed or endured, have done, and have dreamed of doing' (p. 2, emphasis added). These powerful pictures of the world are deemed to instil in students who engage with them the politically correct values mentioned earlier. Thus, the approved social ethos is reinforced by infusing the curriculum with these new and different literary pictures of the world; so, a curriculum policy which subscribes to the Arnoldian dictum that literature is an intrinsic civilizing force, yet which feels the need to tailor this principle to the attainment of culturally specific norms, ignores the likelihood that the power of literature will generate a counter-reaction when real students read real texts.

While the humanism of an ever-widening pluralist canon may be theoretically appealing, the limits on the time and resources of educators make it impossible to teach everything. Furthermore, given that most teachers have been trained in the old humanist canon and under the discipline of the poetics of detachment to a sensibility for 'literary context', it is simply naïve to suppose that there should be no conflict over the 'old' humanist world picture and the 'new' world pictures geared to changing cultural realities. If the students in the *Lord of the Flies* example had asked for the addition of a book sympathetic to blacks rather than for the removal of Golding's novel, the issue might have escaped the censorship label, but it would not have avoided the inevitable truth that the very existence of a particular curriculum is vested with social and political authority. In the school text censorship debate, this makes the line between justification and censorship, enculteration and indoctrination, uncomfortably fine.

The 'how' of literature education: pedagogies of engagement and detachment

The romanticizing of literary engagement at the expense of critical detachment exacerbates the split between transformation and enculteration, and hoists literature educators on their own humanist petard in the censorship debate. Notions of literature as 'an inspiring record' of human achievement and 'engagement with the text' both espouse the hope and promise of literature as the embodiment of values to be communicated to and presumably 'caught' by the reader. That literature influences powerfully is the very reason that *what* is read matters within an educational context. If content did not count, there would never be felt the need to change the syllabus nor to move to a response model of pedagogy to make that content palpably real. Thus, the literary engagement model, described above, is not predicated on the educational value of literature as timeless or self-evident, irrespective of its content; rather, it assumes that literature does and should influence in specific directions. Yet the rhetoric of curriculum guidelines would persuade us that the 'power' of literature is intrinsically and innocently empowering to the student, that absorption, getting lost in a text, inhabiting fictional worlds and identifying with fictional characters sympathetically is a major tenet of literature's educational value. This educational double-speak – the timeless educational value of literature, on the one hand, and the stated goal that literature influences in certain socially relevant directions, on the other – reflects the humanist tradition's in-built diremptive tendency, a tendency previously held in check by the concern of literary education with only one cultural heritage, and a poetics that determined and constituted what would be an educated response to that heritage. It seems that educators still feel the value of 'literary context' as the important element in the education/ transformation of the reader, but have failed to realize that it was the politics of the hegemony and the poetics of detachment that made this education unproblematic.

As already stated, one of the tenets of the engagement model is that literary experience is a form of 'real' experience, the beneficial educational effects of which are unquestioned (Rosenblatt, 1978). Like the civilizing power of literature, identification and relevance, engagement has been a given of the moral value of literature on the assumption that readers resonate with verbal facsimiles of reality experienced as the feeling of coming to know certain 'truths' about themselves and/or the world. Here Shelley's dictum that 'Poets are the unacknowledged legislators of the world' seems unassailable. Literary education has historically taken on the mantle, awesome in its responsibility, for powerful self-transformations in student readers. One of the reasons why censorship is such a thorny issue at present is that the assumed goal of literature education – personal growth and transformation – has finally come into its own through the engagement model. However, the trajectory of such change is highly unpredictable. Not surprisingly, then, some students and parents find that strong literary works can be threatening. It has ever been thus, but formerly a pedagogy of detachment, i.e. the *study* of literature, provided a container for the discomfiting effects of imaginative identity. Without that container, students can be either left on their own to battle self-alienation or saddled with an anaemic curriculum expunged of any genuine human encounter.

Often literature educators do not readily acknowledge that engagement and identification cut both ways: they can induce alienation as well as produce validation. Rather, when faced with the prospect of a work which engages readers so as to alienate them, we often defend that work on other grounds, thereby denying the importance of engagement as redemptive in literary experience. Consequently, denial that reading literature entails a 'descent' into unconscious forces as a precondition for individuated identity is at the heart of rationales *for* teaching some works whereas affirmation of 'descent' fuels rationales *against* teaching others. Typically, denial is rationalized through the employment of a detachment model, the most widely used strategy for retaining an indicted book on the curriculum being the appeal to literary context and the distinction between literature and life (Dick, 1982). However, the apologists would collapse that distinction when lobbying for their own literary content and the values it is thought to propound (Ontario Ministry of Education, 1987). The response model of literary engagement, in making tangible literary experience, simply reinforces the inconsistency in the two lines of argument in the justification and censorship problems. In the case of *Lord of the Flies*, the English department knew they could not have it both ways: to take seriously literature's transformational function in empowering students to be responsible for their own learning and to deny those students access to the power of choice.

By a pedagogy of detachment, I do not intend a return to formal analysis (though there is no intrinsic reason why literary criticism should inhibit literary experience), but education for critical consciousness (Freire, 1960) through locating literary works in their historical context (Robinson, 1987), inquiring into the constructed nature of literary language (Belsey, 1980), as well as developing strategies for scrutinizing the conditions – personal, moral, aesthetic, social and political – of response (Scholes, 1985; Robinson, 1987; Thomson, 1987). A pedagogy of detachment might have afforded the students objecting to *Lord of the Flies* the opportunity to study the basis for their protest by deconstructing (Culler, 1982) those literary-educational values – sympathetic identification, social relevance, literary quality, transformation and enculteration – which furnished the grounds for its presence on the syllabus. This kind of inquiry is no less important in literature than it is in media literacy, the latter now recognized as a basic educational need (Ontario Ministry of Education, 1987). It is just this awareness of the conditions of literary response upon which my conception of 'literary literacy' rests (see also Mares, 1988).

Literary literacy and the meta-problem

I hope that a comprehensive definition of literary literacy, encompassing the implications of the direct, participating response and the self-consciousness of the critical response, would provide a heuristic to help us maintain consistency in drafting rationales *for* teaching literature and *against* the censorship of particular literary works, to acknowledge the political investment in any literature curriculum, and to prepare for conflicts that will inevitably sacrifice someone's 'imaginative heaven' on the altar of someone else's 'imaginative hell'. A pedagogy of engagement which legitimates subjective response cannot logically support exhortations to offended readers not to *feel* a certain way – the author's intention, historical and/or literary context, and the need to preserve a cultural heritage notwithstanding. A pedagogy of critical detachment will not solve this 'mortification' aspect of the censorship dilemma, but it can provide a conceptual framework for literary experience. Emotional connection and imaginative identity with a poem or story lend to literature its ineffability, without which it would simply not be literature. However, so long as educators continue to credit this aspect of literature with educational value, we can no longer blink at the principle of the double effect of the text.

What, then, are we to do? One solution might be to supplant a pedagogy of engagement with that of detachment; but that would eclipse the aesthetic dimension of the literary enterprise and counteract the recognition by other educational domains, such as critical pedagogy, of 'identification' over 'reason' (Scahill, 1989: 96) so crucial to altering perception and attitudes. This brings us full circle to the fundamental problem of the meta-problem – the definition of literature itself. If literature is something other than a social document or philosophical proposition, then its aesthetic dimension must be logically prior to its ratiocinative value. If the unpredictable effects of literary engagement are neutralized by an over-self-consciousness of response, then we risk reifying literature by keeping it separate from life.

However, the painful choice between the fusion of literature and life, and a pedagogy of engagement on the one hand, and the separation of literature and life, and a pedagogy of detachment on the other, is unnecessary. Literary literacy should embrace both engagement and detachment, both the feeling of coming to know certain 'truths' about oneself and/or the world, and getting distance on that feeling. As such, it would enable students to read literature as assertion, as a form of knowing and as hypothesis, as a form of questioning. I do not expect that even the attainment of such a Utopian goal would be a panacea in the censorship issue, for curricula, like literature, have the power to influence for good and ill. Their authority to include and exclude particular voices or points of view defines the relationship of even the most literate student to the political landscape shaping cultural studies. For those who are marginalized, such a defining can be the experience of alienation. Thus, awareness of the political context of the engaged reader might be a necessary first step in respecting one another's imaginative and psychological identities, and in coming to grips with the meta-problem. If cultural literacy (Hirsch, 1987) is to be truly emancipatory, it must acknowledge patterns of dominance and control of the culture, where justification and censorship become two sides of a coin flipped all too often in favour of privilege. A definition of literary literacy might help keep the odds even.

Let us conclude by returning to *Lord of the Flies*. Was the English department in that instance practising censorship in abdicating responsibility for transmitting the cultural heritage or was it practising what it preached by respecting the dignity of minorities, and nurturing their individual and collective identities? I believe it was doing both. What it did *not* do was evade the lived experience of the students in front of them under the cloak of an abstract principle. This took courage, especially in the face of liberal notions of unfettered entitlement to knowledge regardless of its cost in human sensibility. Again, I do not advocate capitulating to pressure groups at the expense of the entire Western tradition of liberal thought, but if knowledge is inscribed with bias, as I believe it is, if education is implicated in that bias, and if educational policy continues to enshrine the power of literary knowledge in advancing the cause of 'concerned truth' (Frye, 1971: 66), then the tension between espousing that concern and the freedom to pursue it must be held before it can ever be resolved, if it can be resolved at all. Holding the tension means attending to the exigencies of the asymmetrical relationship between the dominant and the marginalized, between those who would know, the 'heroes' of the intellectual quest and those who provide the ground for that quest. Ideally, these two roles will ultimately be exchanged on the journey to enlightenment, in which every voice eventually resonates as part of one's own. However, that time has not yet come. So those in control can afford to relinquish some control, giving pride of place in the curriculum to what is 'other', to new stories and different voices.

Lord of the Flies has not disappeared from the curriculum; it has merely taken a well-earned rest, but there is no mistaking that at least in one school, the novel is a casualty – welcome or unwelcome – of the honest expression of some problems inherent in the logic of inclusion and exclusion. Meanwhile, the key players in the Toronto controversy have reached a proto-typically Canadian compromise solution. *Lord of the Flies* has been officially reinstated (see 'School board rejects bid to ban novel', *The Globe and Mail*, 1 July 1988). The indicted book continues to be compulsory reading in eight Toronto schools, and the conflict has resulted in a number of positive recommendations:

1 Teachers should be allowed to decide whether or not to use the book.
2 A rationale for the withdrawal of *Lord of the Flies* should be circulated to all schools.
3 The Board should ask its committee on bias in the curriculum to determine 'how the book could be suitably used'.
4 Teachers should be trained 'in the selection and use of novels'.
5 Money should be provided for replacing 'biased books'.

(The Globe and Mail, 1 July 1988)

The political implementation of literary literacy has, then, already begun; it is hoped that a theory of literary literacy would help make practising it logically consistent, epistemologically sound and socially equitable. As for the great tradition of arts and letters, Shelley can surely rest content that no longer are poets the *un*acknowledged legislators of the world.

7 Information books in the primary school: the language of action or reflection?

ALISON LITTLEFAIR

There is concern among teachers, publishers, writers and researchers that interesting, meaningful information books should be available for young readers. Not only is this a response to the National Curriculum, but there is increased understanding that readers should experience a range of types of writing.

Publishers and writers are at the forefront of producing texts which introduce young readers to non-narrative writing. Their task is not easy, for the simplification of the language of information is a complex undertaking. However, it seems timely to consider the strategies which are used and their likely effectiveness in widening young children's awareness of more formal writing.

Reading standards

This publishing activity is taking place amid a great deal of public criticism of the teaching of reading. We are only too aware that both quality and popular newspapers have seized upon the question of the standards of the reading achievement of seven-year-old pupils in schools. I have no intention of debating the merits of a 'phonic approach' or a 'real books' approach to teaching reading. Rather, I am concerned with another aspect of reading development, that of the development of pupils' ability to read 'all types of writing', the focus of the target for Reading in the National Curriculum for state schools in England and Wales.

The present debate is about the initial teaching of reading. A report by Her Majesty's Inspectors of Education (DES, 1990: 6iii) states that about three-quarters of the children assessed could read with accuracy and understanding by the age of seven. About half had progressed to become fluent readers. The question has to be asked, therefore, why a percentage of seemingly promising readers had *not* progressed to fluency.

This finding is not surprising if we consider previous research which has suggested that many children do not continue to develop their reading in ways which enable them to read with understanding the more subject specific texts which they meet in the secondary school.

Over ten years ago, Lunzer and Gardner (1979) spoke of a 'retreat from print' and gave staggeringly low figures – in seconds – of the time spent in reading by the secondary school pupils they observed. More recently, Open University researchers (Chapman, 1987) made a longitudinal study of 1500 pupils for a three-year period. At the beginning of the survey the three age-bands of the pupils were eight, ten and thirteen years. The researchers noted that the children of lower reading ability and possibly some of average reading ability had a serious reading problem as they proceeded up the secondary school. The implication is that many children in the secondary school find reading a variety of texts to be problematic. My own research (Littlefair, 1991) suggests that awareness of register is developmental and an important factor in children's reading development.

Jeanne Chall and colleagues (1990) reported research into the reading development of children of 'low economic status'. She indicated that the children who were able to read with meaning in Grade 3 began to slip in Grade 4. We might, at this point, note that two important factors suggested by Chall are awareness of different linguistic structures and the importance of a wide vocabulary.

In the light of these findings, we should extend any debate about reading beyond the initial stages of 'learning to read' to the question of the development of competence to read **flexibly**.

The reading curriculum

If we are to help pupils to read a range of writing with understanding, we must plan a broad reading curriculum which spans from the infant school to the secondary school and provides for a balanced experience of all types of books.

As Michael Marland notes (1991), the National Curriculum does not provide a detailed curriculum for reading. It states that pupils are to be able to read 'all types of writing', but we are left to work out just how the junior and secondary schools are to plan the teaching of relevant skills and concepts so that children will be in a position to read with meaning the varied texts which will confront them as they proceed through school.

On the whole, children learn to read stories and become familiar with the way in which they are written. They are not so familiar with the way in which *non*-fiction books are written. The emphasis on narrative in the primary school is replaced in the secondary schools by increasing demands to read for study purposes. Of course, the switch from narrative to factual texts is not so stark. For some time, junior school pupils have engaged in topic work mainly in order to have experience of finding and recording information from books, but we should consider whether this reading activity sufficiently prepares pupils to read with understanding the more formal language of explanation, description, argument and instructions.

If pupils are to read a range of writing competently, they should have the opportunity to read and listen to extended texts of factual writing as well as searching for information by use of reading strategies such as skimming and scanning. As Margaret Meek says (1988: 21):

> The most important single lesson that children learn from texts is the nature and variety of written discourse, the different ways that a language lets a writer tell, and the many and different ways a reader reads.

Perhaps, first, we have to become more aware of the ways of expression of different genres of writing.

What do we mean by 'genres'?

We are quite familiar with the use of 'genre' when it relates to categories of written communications. We choose a genre form which is appropriate for a purpose. For instance, if we wish to write to a solicitor we write a formal letter. If we are asked to review a recently published book for a journal, we write a book review. We probably keep a diary if we wish to record our impressions of a journey.

Some linguists give the word 'genre' a much broader definition. They describe 'genres' as social processes in which we engage as members of a culture. Social processes follow characteristic patterns. There are, for instance, descriptions of the patterns of spoken communications we follow when we visit shops (Halliday and Hasan, 1989; Ventola, 1987), or when we make an appointment to visit the doctor's surgery (Hasan, 1978). In other words, genres are seen as being the ways in which we create meaning in our culture. This is a development of Hallidayan thinking about the ways in which language varies according to context. Any spoken or written communication has a characteristic pattern which varies according to purpose and situation.

Categorizing books

In the same way, genres of writing display characteristic organization and can be categorized on the basis of writers' purposes; the range of reading which children meet throughout their school careers can also be categorized on the basis of writers' general purposes.

Books where the writer's purpose is to narrate and/or to express personal response can be placed within the **literary** genre; where the writer's purpose is to explain, describe, give information objectively or persuasively can be placed within the **expository** genre; where the writer's purpose is to give instructions, within the **procedural** genre. (My use of the term 'reference books' is, therefore, limited to those books where the writer's purpose is to give brief, easily accessed information.) Of course, these are very broad categories, each of which has many sub-categories or genres. Nor can we strictly compartmentalize these genres, for they may well overlap. For example, reference books, as described here, are often organized as a list of items, but each item may well be explained in the language of explanation and description. This is in contrast to the more usual practice in schools of categorizing books according to their subject matter. It is also in contrast to such publishers' categories as:

- 'reading/language scheme' books;
- 'trade books' sold to book shops;
- 'resource books' (which sometimes refers to books used by pupils for topic work);
- 'text books' (which sometimes refers to subject-specific books used in the primary school).

In addition, terms like 'factual', 'non-fiction', 'reference' and 'information' books are very general categories which we all use quite appropriately. None of these categories, however, differentiates between different kinds of linguistic expression which appear in non-fiction book genres.

Language within genres

A writer chooses the genre which is suitable for his or her purpose and within that genre form chooses a register of language deemed to be appropriate to express meaning.

The register usually chosen by writers of stories for young children is one which is close to their readers' experience of language in their everyday lives. The grammar of the sentences will be fairly simple and not too removed from their readers' experience of spoken language. The content of the story probably relates to their readers' common sense knowledge. Most young readers will be carried along by the dynamics of the actions of the characters. I refer to this register as the **language of action**.

As I have already noted, research suggests that we cannot assume that competent readers of fiction and its language of action will become competent readers of fact. Indeed, Margaret Donaldson (1989) asserts that if children's reading experience consists mainly of stories, there is little chance of their simply picking up more objective language.

The register of many factual books is that of explanation, description, instructions and questioning. Explanatory and descriptive writing present immediate difficulties. The subject matter may be outside the reader's experience and so there will be little feeling of personal involvement. There will be increasing demands for reflection, for writers of expository text present not only information, but ideas and ways of thinking.

The National Curriculum for English refers to chronological and non-chronological texts. Events in a story are usually arranged in some kind of chronological order, whereas the organization of an expository text is probably based on a logical arrangement such as cause and effect, problem and solution, comparison and contrast. As expository books become more sophisticated, the vocabulary becomes increasingly subject-specific and far removed from the reader's vocabulary. Also sentences become longer, including far more content words than those which have a purely grammatical function. The large number of content words has the effect of 'packing' meaning into sentences. The reverse happens in conversation and many stories written for young children include lots of conversation. In expository texts the main action of a sentence often comes after a complex introduction. The cohesion between sections of text becomes more complex and may be subject-specific. The writer may set up a degree of remoteness by using such grammatical devices as the passive voice and create further formality by using the third person. As they read more sophisticated expository texts, pupils will meet increasing use of abstract language.

Margaret Donaldson (1989) describes such language as that of 'systematic thought' and as 'a sub-class of the language of books'. She emphasizes the importance of children being introduced to such language not only to increase their familiarity with it, but also to extend their powers of thinking beyond their own personal involvements.

> They need to learn gradually, over the school years, how to participate in the impersonal mode of thinking and of linguistic expression that are such an important part of our cultural heritage.   (Donaldson, 1989: 25)

Of course, most very young readers cannot be plunged into this kind of expression, but it would seem to be of the greatest importance that factual books are written in ways which will commence an awareness of more impersonal writing than that found in story books. We certainly should not allow our young readers to wander into the realms of reading factual books without adequate preparation.

So writers and publishers are faced with a complex task. How is explanatory and descriptive language, in particular, to be simplified for these young readers? How can we produce early non-fiction books so that young readers experience language which is a reasonable introduction to the way in which expository genres are written?

The question of mixed genres

I have already noted that young children's reading is principally in the powerful genre of narrative in which their interest is engaged in following the actions of characters through a vocabulary which is usually fairly familiar and simple grammatical constructions. Here is language which bridges something of the gap between spoken and written language and content, which is imaginative and creative, which probably relates to familiar activities and which is generally appealing. We can say that stories are child-centred since they are directed towards pupils' interest and, in this way, a vital context is created within which children learn to read.

This concern to provide a meaningful context also influences the writing of factual books for very young children. The result of this concern is that many authors mix fact with fiction as they write factual books for young readers. Thus, we find non-fiction books which:

- introduce human characters;
- introduce direct speech;
- personify animals, plants, etc.;
- arrange the text as a story;
- are written in the form of poems.

I want to ask whether these strategies are appropriate. It may well be argued that, in order to avoid giving young readers unfamiliar texts too suddenly, we should mediate by placing information within the more familiar genre of narrative and thus create a link between the known story form and the less familiar forms of other genres. On the other hand, if the purpose of these books is to introduce young readers to other kinds of written expression of meaning, then these strategies do not seem so appropriate.

Fact and fiction are different kinds of meaning which are expressed in ways which have evolved within our culture. As sophisticated users of language, we recognize those ways and, as we educate children, we introduce them to a range of ways of thinking and ways of representing the world we live in. So, as we teach reading and writing we introduce pupils to ways in which we express meaning through written language. If we do less than this, then as educators we fail to pass on essential knowledge.

Early information books

Many information books published for young readers are written as simple introductions to scientific subjects and illustrate the search for a suitable way of introducing readers to factual language. Often these books are found within a reading/language scheme and are advertised as an introduction to non-fiction writing, although they obviously also have a principal purpose of extending young pupils' understanding of the world around them.

In a paper given at the 1990 World Congress on Reading, Unsworth (1990) notes the temptation for writers of early science books simply to report everyday happenings rather than grasp the nettle of introducing young readers to the beginnings of scientific understanding. Of course, children must be able to see a link between their everyday experiences and scientific theory, but scientists endeavour to explain and order the world, not through narrative, but through another kind of discourse. So, in terms of content, we are faced with the problem of how to link common sense and theoretical knowledge, and how we should express these new ideas linguistically. How do we extend pupils' understanding and, at the same time, introduce them to the language of description and explanation? As Unsworth notes, how is scientific language to be recontextualized for young readers? We have to think about the images we create if, for instance, we talk about white cells 'eating up' germs.

As children begin to talk and read about science they must surely begin to move away from their everyday world to more detached scientific thinking. Sometimes scientific knowledge may even challenge common sense knowledge. For example, we commonly think of tomatoes as vegetables, whereas scientifically they are fruits. As Martin (1990) says of these two kinds of knowledge, 'They are different pictures of reality and we have to construct reasonable links between the two views.'

Strube (1990) describes the use of narrative in the late nineteenth century as a means of introducing scientific ideas to children. Characters in a narrative would discuss scientific concepts in a way which was seen as a practical and entertaining way of helping pupils widen their understanding. However, when this idea is taken and used now as the basis for writing about the world around us for very young children, a range of strategies appears, as has already been noted. Some writers describe plants and animals as though they were people. Personifying the subjects they are writing about seems to be an attempt to suggest that young pupils can understand aspects of the world around them only in the terms of a story and probably underestimates the capability of most children.

The logical development from personifying animals and plants is to imagine the kind of conversation which might take place. Of course, the advantage of direct speech will be seen to be its close relationship with oral spoken language.

'This is my tree,'
said the bee.

'This is my tree,'
said the ladybird.
(Cutting and Cutting, 1988: 8–9)

Sometimes the writer changes the register and, therefore, the kind of meaning being expressed quite radically. This extract, for example, uses the formal language of information:

Every morning as the sun rises in Africa,
the animals come down to their water-hole,
(Elliot, 1989: 2)

but later in the text the register becomes that of conversation:

> 'Well,' say the hippos,
> 'we can't live in a cage either.
> We might look heavy
> but we can run faster than a man.
> We like to spend most of our time in water.'
> (Elliot, 1989: 14)

Here the writer seems to be using conversation as the vehicle of explanation, which seems a contradiction if the purpose is to introduce explanatory language.

Again, in the following extract, the writer has introduced a formal register, but has introduced conversation as though some personalizing of the information must be included if children are to learn about things which may be outside their experience.

> The vet visits a koala.
> It is time for his injection.
> The keepers coax
> the koala down from
> his tree top, then hold
> him firmly for the vet.
>
> Afterwards he scrambles back among the gum leaves.
> 'I'm glad that's over!'.
> (Brennan and Keaney, 1988)

Here there are other problems. For example, this text has the chronological organization of a narrative, which does not seem to be an effective way of introducing non-chronological texts.

Several writers choose to involve human characters within a story setting. The purpose of this approach has little to do with introducing the young reader to different types of text, but rather to extend the reader's understanding of a scientific concept in a way which is seen as 'reader friendly'. Yet again, there is a tendency for these strategies to lead to chronologically arranged texts. This is possibly a view of educational knowledge which suggests that objectivity is to be avoided; the emphasis in the text is on an arbitrary character and, therefore, on the everyday world rather than on the purpose of drawing the reader's attention towards more scientific thinking.

If factual books are written to extend pupils' interest in reading and to be a 'halfway house' between fact and fiction, they may not be suitable for use in information retrieval activities. Bobby Neate (1990) has made similar observations about texts which she terms 'children's anomalous texts'. It is difficult to locate information from a text where the content is subject-specific, but the organization of the text is that of a narrative.

There may well be early non-fiction books which are written with the purpose of promoting the readers' enjoyment. There would not be any other reason for the following extract which comes from a book about festivals which is written in the form of a free-verse poem!

Spring brings Holi, the festival of colours,
A Hindu celebration.
Bonfires are lit, coloured water thrown. Accept the invitation!
(McLeay, 1987: 3)

Elsewhere, the same author writes to give some information as well as to provide amusement.

Small plant pots are all you need,
And compost soft to house the seed.

Cover with an old glass jar,
Find a cupboard, not too far ...
(McLeay 1986: 5)

If we accept the argument that a mixed genre is appropriate for young readers, we still have to help our readers cope with genuine expository and procedural texts.

The purpose of a series of popular science books for young pupils is stated as introducing, 'young children to science in an informed and enjoyable way' (Jennings, 1989). This is, of course, a reasonable purpose, but we must ask **when** children are to begin to read about science in a more impersonal way. At some point, young readers should have the experience of reading and listening to language which provides an introduction to non-chronological arrangement of text and increasingly impersonal ways of expression as in this extract:

The baby frog-hoppers breathe air through their mouths.
The air passes right through their bodies
and out at the other end.
The sap, the wax and the air
all come out of their bodies as bubbles.
The bubbles look rather like washing-up liquid.
But the frog-hoppers don't wash with it.
They use it to keep themselves cool and moist
while they feed on the plants and grow up.
(Arnold, 1990: 17)

This extract is immediately followed by conversation between two human characters. We should urgently consider whether there is need to create a narrative context for very young readers as they read expository text.

Information books for older juniors

Books in the factual genres have been written for older junior pupils for some time. A review of recent publications reveals many books where the writers have endeavoured to present less familiar forms of expression which children will meet in subject texts used in the secondary school. Writers of these books frequently include more than one genre. Sometimes the different genres are signalled by use of different type or are placed within different sections of the book, which may be indicated by different coloured paper.

These two extracts from a book about oil rigs are examples of writing in the register of both expository and procedural genres.

Looking at rocks

Oil explorers have to find out all they can about the layers of rock under the land and sea. The layers may have been bent, cracked or shifted by movements of the surface of the Earth. If so, oil or gas may have collected inside the rock.

Geologists are the experts who can see, by studying rocks, whether they are likely to contain oil or gas. Pictures of the land taken from planes or satellites show the patterns of rock formations down below. Geologists also examine the rocks under the sea bed.   (Ardley, 1989: 12)

The language is that of explanation and description – the beginning of reflective language. The organization of the text is logical rather than sequential. For instance, the phrase 'layers of rock' is followed by an explanation as to why oil might have formed within them. The work of a geologist is briefly described. This is not the more expressive language of stories, but it is accessible to young readers: the sentences are reasonably short and the grammar is not too unfamiliar, even though it includes restricted use of the passive voice. On the opposite page is a register of language within a procedural genre.

Searching for magnetic rocks

You will need: a small magnet, a sheet of newspaper, a plastic cup, a metal object (paper clip or safety pin), and a partner.
1 Put the metal object in the bottom of the plastic cup.
2 Tell your partner not to look. Put the magnet under the newspaper.
3 Your partner is now the geologist and has to find the magnet. Holding the cup one centimetre above the paper, your partner should move it across the newspaper, in straight lines. When the metal object twitches, jumps or twists, then the magnetic 'rock' has been found.   (Ardley, 1989: 13)

After an initial grouping of items, the arrangement of the language is quite different. There are numbered items in a list. Each item is a command. A sense of personal involvement is maintained by use of the second person as in 'You will need . . .'.

I suggest that it is appropriate to include these two genres in the book, for each expresses the writer's purpose of explanation and then of instruction, and each is clearly differentiated.

Writing of the narrative genre and of the expository genre may be found in the same information book. In this case, however, the narrative is not contrived, since it is a retelling of a legend:

Odysseus' passion for hunting once almost cost him his life. Some years earlier
he had been savagely gored by a wild boar, and the wound had left a ragged
scar above his knee. But this had not put him off. He was a superb marksman
and would sometimes display his skill by shooting an arrow through a line of
twelve axes without hitting one of them.   (Connolly, 1986: 4)

Here the register of language is that of a story. There are colloquial expressions, such as 'cost him his life' and 'put him off' which heighten the
reader's sense of familiarity with the language. Striking adverbs and
adjectives, such as, 'savagely', 'ragged' and 'superb', heighten the impression
of action. The vocabulary is not always that of familiar conversation, but the
reader is assisted by fairly simple cohesive devices and, of course, the whole
passage has sequential organization which is indicated by use of 'some years
earlier' and 'once'.

In a separate section of the same book, made obvious by different page
arrangements and different print, we find the language of explanation and
description:

A Golden Age

The legend of Odysseus is based on the two earliest pieces of European literature, the Illiad and the Odyssey. These two epic poems are believed to have
been composed by the Greek poet Homer some time in the 8th century BC.
They tell of a Golden Age long before the poet's time and of the heroes who
fought in the legendary Trojan War.   (Connolly, 1986: 12)

This writing which reflects upon the origin of the legend is fairly formal.
The writer has introduced the passive voice, but has not written lengthy
introductions to sentences. There is less familiar vocabulary; indeed, many
terms may need explanation.

The question of narrative in information books for older readers continues
to be problematic. Vivien Griffiths (1990) refers to a 'narrative approach' in
her report of the 'Times Educational Supplement' Junior Information Book
Awards for 1990. Her example is the authentic story of a boy during the
Second World War who:

... tells his story in a chatty informal style which brings the period alive for the
reader. This is an imaginative treatment of a familiar period of history and gives
an excellent example of the use of primary sources for the young researcher.

On the other hand, she refers to 'story format', the sudden appearance of
narrative writing in an information book.

An example of such an appearance of narrative is in a history book where
the informal description of Celtic life suddenly bursts into an imaginary situation where the reader is depicted as talking to two Celtic children within a
farmhouse. The writer's purpose is probably to engage the interest of the
reader, but in doing so, he has abandoned the way in which explanations are
expressed.

As teachers, we have to decide how and when we are to prepare pupils for the formal, abstract language of subject texts across the curriculum. We might consider the involved sentences in the quotation below.

The River Cam, which flows through the City of Cambridge, was once much wider and surrounded by swampy land. If people or animals tried to cross they sank into bog and sometimes drowned. But they soon discovered a place where two ridges of land came right down to the edge of the river, where they could wade across without too much danger. Gradually, houses were built beside this fording place and much later, a bridge was made, giving the present city its name.

To the north-east of Cambridge was a huge area of undrained fenland. It was very difficult to cross this desolate marsh as there were no known tracks. In the battles which continually took place over the centuries, an army holding the crossing place at Cambridge was in a strong position to repel its enemy.

(Graham-Cameron, 1977: 2)

Not only must young readers become familiar with extended texts of explanatory and descriptive language, but they must also become aware of a range of ways in which information is organized. Christie and Rothery (1990) stress the importance of children beginning to learn how to 'find their way' round books and to know something about the different kinds of discourse used in a range of subjects.

Researchers (Eggins *et al.*, 1987) looked at a number of history and geography texts in Australian high schools. They found emphasis in history books not to be on narrative, but increasingly on the arrangement, interpretation and generalization of events. The emphasis in geography texts was found to be on grouping and classifying of items, and on analysis and explanation. This means that writers are putting some kind of order onto aspects of the world which children learn about. Text books about geography also include taxonomies which are often indicated by chapter headings and subheadings. Of course, this kind of arrangement of text is even more apparent in later writing about science.

Texts for junior school readers such as the following extract provide an excellent introduction to these arrangements of text:

The Thermosphere
The air in the thermosphere is extremely thin.
Temperatures in this layer of the atmosphere can reach as high as 2000°C.

The Mesophere
The mesophere lies between 48 and 80 kilometres from the Earth's surface. Extremely strong winds blow in this section and trails of hot gas from burning meteorites can be seen.

(Carter *et al.*, 1990: 7)

Implications of developing awareness of reflective language

Genre forms are not rigid, however, for we gradually alter them as our purposes and perceptions change. New purposes encourage the development of ways in which we speak and write. If at the end of the twentieth century we want to enable our young readers to have an easy transition from reading sequential stories to more logically arranged explanations, descriptions and instructions then perhaps we are searching for a new genre. Our purpose must be clear. We have to look at a continuum which bridges informal expression to formal expression without losing sight of the fact that we are writing about the factual world.

A developmental approach is essential, for we should not forget other implications which are involved in an awareness of more reflective language. Children who do not easily acquire competency with more impersonal language may well have difficulty in developing the kind of intellectual abilities which they require if they are to cope with schooling and with many of the demands of adult life.

James Paul Gee (1991: 130) speaks of 'essay-text literacy'. He suggests that claims for a link between competence in 'essay-text literacy' and the development of thinking are valid only within a western context. None the less, Gee notes the worldwide influence of this kind of literacy and, hence, the importance of children being introduced to it. He refers to teachers, and English teachers in particular, as 'gatekeepers' who must give pupils the opportunity to have 'control over the discourse practices in thought, speech and writing of essay-text literacy and its attendant world view.'

We are right to be concerned about how we introduce more formal language to young pupils. Not only must they be in a position to manage the later literacy demands of our society, but they should be able to manipulate their literacy skills for their own purposes. We cannot leave it to chance, for as Margaret Donaldson (1989: 27) warns

The ability to deal with sophisticated impersonal prose ... does not leap up suddenly when needed like the genie from Aladdin's lamp. It is the outcome of years of sustained direction towards an ultimate goal. If primary teachers do not recognise this they are failing to see the scope and reach of their own importance.

8 New demands on the model for writing in education – what does genre theory offer?

JOHN DIXON AND LESLIE STRATTA

The need for a new model

It is roughly twenty-five years since James Moffett (1968), the London Writing Research Team (Britton *et al.*, 1975), James Kinneavy (1971) and others set out to produce their new models for writing. That magnificent survivor, the tradition of eighteenth century Scottish rhetoric, was at last being toppled. The key categories of Exposition, Argument, Description and Narration were due for a major transformation – which is not to say we do not see many vestiges still around, fogging the issues.

There were strengths in all this work of a generation ago, as we shall be showing, but there were also limitations, some of which were acknowledged. What is more, over these twenty-five years there have been great strides in our understanding of teaching and learning within the classroom. Students' and teachers' roles have changed: they have become jointly responsible for what goes on – and we can see more fully how talking and listening, drama, writing and reading feed one into the other. In some classrooms, teaching and learning has become a dialogic process.

If we are right, this implies a new model for classroom language within which writing has an integral role, not as an isolated end in itself, but as part of an intricate social web of making meanings and organizing practices. What writing leads into, and what arises from it, has to be part of any new model.

In England and Wales the demand has a particular urgency. Their National Curriculum calls for classrooms 'where, individually and collaboratively' pupils are seen to be:

Acknowledgements We would like to acknowledge the help we have had from discussion with Ken Watson and from the articles he has written in collaboration with Wayne Sawyer [see Reid (1987) and Christie and Rothery (1989) and Christie *et at.* (1989) *English in Australia* 1989/90].

- using language to make, receive and communicate meaning, in purposeful contexts;
- employing a variety of forms with a clear awareness of audience;
- working on tasks which they have chosen and which they direct for themselves . . .   (Cox Report, 3.4; DES, 1988a)

By the age of 16 the target is for 'the following range of functions' to be under fluent control:

reporting, narrating, persuading, arguing, describing, instructing, explaining
. . .
recollecting, organising thoughts, reconstructing, reviewing, hypothesising . . .
                                         (Cox Report, 17.46, DES, 1988a)

Given the threat of a curriculum which is open to political manipulation, it is important to recognize the emphases here on collaborative work, on pupil autonomy, on making and communicating meaning, and on the interrelationship between writer and reader. Nevertheless, we want to ask whether that specific range of functions was theoretically based and justifiable.

An Australian alternative

Looking around internationally, we can see one group who, during the past ten years, have been making a sustained effort to shape an alternative model of writing. This Australian group of linguists and educationists seems to have been central: Frances Christie, Joan Rothery, Gunther Kress and Jim Martin. In this paper, we want to consider what can be learnt, both positively and negatively, from their work to date.

The group starts from a criticism of current classroom practices, as they see them:

The whole movement toward child-centred education has foundered on the idea that children can understand and undertake history, geography and other subject areas 'in their own words'. That this is a necessary starting point, no-one would deny, especially not those interested in genre-based approaches to writing development. But that children should be stranded there, writing stories for example as their only genre in infant and primary school, is impossible to accept. It cuts them off absolutely from any real understanding of what the humanities, social sciences and sciences are on about and denies them the tools these disciplines have developed to understand the world.   (Reid, 1987: 64)

Schooling values certain genres more than others, they continue, and 'among those genres of greatest importance for school learning [are] the various factual genres':

These include reports, explanations and expositions, and about these we are in a position to say a great deal of their linguistic organisation . . .

> Without the capacity to handle the written genres in which information is processed and understood in the contemporary world, people will be truly left out, unable to participate in a world of increasingly sophisticated information, construction and exchange.   (Christie and Rothery, 1989: 6, 9)

Denying access to genres disables people socially; and conversely, giving them access to genres must, apparently, empower them.

In some respects we can sympathize with their alarm, if this is really what is happening in child-centred Australian schools. We had similar feelings ourselves, during the early 1980s, when we were working with chief examiners in English, searching for exemplars of positive achievements in writing at 16+. Despite our access to hundreds of course work folders, we did find it very difficult at first to obtain anything of real quality beyond narrative.

Nevertheless, we had to be careful in weighing up such evidence. Within the overall curriculum for 14–17-year-olds we had little doubt that personal or imaginative narrative was a minor element. Post-14, generalization rules: this has been a long-standing tradition in British schools (Britton *et al.*, 1975: 164). Equally, there have been long-standing efforts within English itself, to ensure that students learn to discuss and argue, for instance, as well as to narrate. Over the past twenty years, vocational colleges have developed many courses in Communication for 16–19-year-olds.

As for social empowerment, we fully agree that, if students are to have more control over events, they must learn to persuade, advise, refute, report, inform, revise, plan, predict, speculate . . . empathize, criticize and so on. Clearly, they must do so, on occasion in writing as well as in speech, but this is not simply a matter of producing generic forms. You have no power as a writer unless what you say has some effect on real people: any social model of writing needs to include a systematic treatment of readers and their response.

The notion of genre has a central place in the model; obviously, we must analyse why that is so.

The effort to define genres

The group has based its notion of genre on its study of the systemic linguistic theories of Michael Halliday.

> Ours is a systemic linguistic theory which holds that language is a resource people use for the construction and negotiation of meaning. The theory holds further that because language is used to build meaning, the people in any given culture develop characteristically patterned ways of using language in order to serve the complex set of functions humans have. Such characteristic patterns, then, are social constructs, fashioned out of the constant and ongoing need of people to organise, control and hence make sense of their world.
>   (Christie and Rothery, 1989: 3–4)

So, characteristically patterned ways of using language are there to be found. In any systemic theory, we assume, each pattern will be defined in terms of its relationships with the others, for as Halliday put it:

> Systemic theory is a theory of meaning as choice, by which a language, or any other semiotic system, is interpreted as networks of interlocking options . . .
>
> (1985: xiv)

However, for genre theory things are not so simple, apparently: it turns out that, despite the supporting linguistic work, there are difficulties in defining a genre. Significantly, when introducing the discussion of written genres in 1982, Gunther Kress conceded: 'I have used the term "genre" in a quite non-technical and non-specific way: "mode of writing" might have been a better term' (Christie *et al.*, p. 125).

By 1984, the definition of genre has progressed: genre is defined in the Deakin Study Guide as 'any staged purposeful cultural activity, and it thus includes oral language genres, as well as written language genres. A genre is characterised by having a schematic structure – a distinctive beginning, middle, and end' (p. 270).

The idea of a 'purposeful activity' seems to us a valuable start for thinking about varieties of writing. It is a big step forward from abstract linguistic formalism. As for 'staged' and 'schematic structures', the assumptions may be more dubious. A 'beginning, middle, and end' certainly occurs in some varieties, such as the agenda for a meeting, but this requirement could also imply something more routine and formulaic than we want to see in school. We have to weigh up how the idea of staged purposes is developed.

One of the difficulties is to know what is meant by a 'stage'. Looking at the Guide in detail (71–3), we find that schematic structures seem to have been defined *ad hoc*. Consider, for example, the following three sentences, each introducing a specified genre:

1 One day my mum bought me some books. (Genre: Observation/Comment.)
2 I saw a bike in the shop.   (Genre: Recount.)
3 I went to the zoo.   (Genre: Recount.)

Each of these opening sentences is given a different structural classification. 1 is classified as an 'observation', 2 as an 'event', and 3 as an 'orientation'. What we need to know is why. This is where we would expect a systemic theory to come into its own. In a sense, all of these seem to us to be 'events', so we want the differences to be pointed out. Unfortunately, no detailed, linguistic analysis of 'staging' is offered. At this point, the classification seems to be simply a matter of the theorist's tacit constructions. However, surely part of the challenge to any systemic theory is to deal with structures beyond the sentence?

Equally serious, we can see problems ahead for the concept of writing as 'purposeful cultural activity'. It is well known that our society offers us many handy ways of construing such purposes: these are expressed in the 'speech act' verbs, the verbs of telling, asking and so on. However, according to Austin, they probably run into thousands (1962). That is rather a lot to handle. Moreover, one cannot assume that for any utterance or text there is a single purpose: careful readers are particularly aware of the problems of sifting multiple, ambiguous purposes.

Linguistics cannot rescue us from this human dilemma. Take any given utterance, such as 'Is the window open?' There is no one-to-one relationship between linguistic signs and speech act or purpose. Context, relative status, paralinguistics, non-verbal signs, all these and more may have to be drawn on, in order to construct a purpose – or purposes.

By 1990 the problem of context was being taken into account by the group. 'Genre' was redefined:

> All language use is context-bound; hence language always occurs as socially meaningful, coherent text, that is, as a particular genre. Given the relative stability of social structures, social situations recur, and the purposes and goals of participants in these situations have a certain regularity, even predictability (for instance, having been to four job-interviews, the fifth one is likely to offer fewer surprises than the first one did). Consequently the texts which 'grow out of' these situations have a certain stability and predictability.
>
> (Macken *et al.*, 1990: Book 1, 7)

Again there are positive developments, potentially at least. The goals of participants have to be considered. (We take it that 'participants' includes both writers and their readers.) This relationship of writers and readers is a problem that the London Writing Research group had a first shot at a generation ago, in their 'sense of audience' categories. Thinking of the teacher-reader, they began to distinguish, in broad terms, a range of roles – starting from the most common at the time, 'teacher as examiner' [Britton *et al.*, 1975: 66]. Teachers as examiners have very narrow goals, obviously. Today, when it comes to reading what is written, we would expect fellow students, teachers and people outside the classroom to be taking on a much wider range of social roles, a task which makes such categorization much more complex.

This recent redefinition of genres also seems to include an important concession about schematic structures. As we interpret it, the phrase 'a certain regularity, even predictablity', allows for a certain non-regularity, even unpredictability.' It is all a matter of degree. For example, consider the 'fifth job interview' mentioned by the group. To our certain knowledge, this 'genre' does not always follow a nice regular, stable pattern. It can last anything from thirty minutes to a couple of days, with simulations, demonstrations, informal discussions with staff and dinner at high table served by college retainers all part of the process.

This example still leaves us a bit uneasy. Even here the group's notion of genre can be far too elastic. Martin, for example, over-extended the use of the term in 1989, listing at one point 'religious ceremonies, participation in political processes, marriage, and so on' and later adding 'genres which attract the attention of the media [including] political marches and rallies, sit-ins, pamphlets, graffiti, sabotage, kidnapping and hijacking . . . (p. 37). Conceived of in this way, a 'staged purposeful cultural activity' turns out to be a Pandora's box. Surely we need something more manageable?

How many genres are there, actually?

In the early days, Kress asserted that:

> Just as there is a small and fixed number of sentence types, so there exists a small and fixed number of genres in any written tradition. The individual can no more create a new genre type than he or she can create a new sentence type.
>
> (1982: 98)

However, by 1987, Kress and the group had modified their stance:

> Genres are dynamic, responding to the dynamics of other parts of social systems. Hence genres change historically; hence new genres emerge over time, and hence, too, what appears as 'the same' generic form at one level has recognizably distinct forms in differing social groups. (1987: 42)

This has vital implications for the classroom. As social relationships and roles in our classrooms change, we teachers must inevitably change both the range of genres – a process we should encourage – and the way each can be constructed.

By 1989, the group had read and analysed 'literally thousands of written texts . . . over all the years of schooling and across most, but not all, school subjects' (p. 5). This is a heroic task, but let us look at some of the categories their group has accepted, presumably as a result of such analysis.

In 1987 Martin et al. listed, among many others, 'jokes, letters to the editor . . . and anecdotes' as genres (p. 59). We find it difficult to imagine a focal purpose and goal for any of these. Letters to the editor may protest, congratulate, offer supporting or conflicting evidence, boast about hearing the first cuckoo, amuse and so on. In fact, Martin says elsewhere that 'the term letter refers to a mode not to a genre . . . As a channel, letters can be used to transmit all kinds of different genres' (1989: 17). This makes sense to us: arguing on these lines, there may be many more 'genres' than the researchers uncovered.

A further question needs to be addressed: are genres single or mixed in purpose? Here, Kress seems to us to have taken a new line. Commenting on an elementary student's writing he says:

What is interesting here is that Joel has produced what is in effect a new generic type . . . The text shows a generic mix, or blend; something not at all unusual in other kinds of texts produced by competent writers or speakers.

(1987: 41)

So there are genres and there are generic blends. If our arithmetic is correct, this must raise the total number exponentially.

To sum up: there seems to be confusion within the group. In 1989, Kress said:

Genre theory in education is not, at this stage, a highly unified body of theory. The contributors to this debate represent a significant range of distinctive positions . . . the debate ranges from a position which treats genres as fully determined in all essential characteristics and therefore as outside the scope for effective individual action, to positions which treat genres as relatively fluid structures, subject to the actions of socially located individual agents.

(1989: 10–11)

How is the theory being implemented in practice?

Here the results are disappointing to date. Consider one instance from work commissioned by the New South Wales Department of Education for Years 3–6 (Macken *et al.*, 1990). This starts by short-listing a range of written genres 'important for participation in both formal schooling and the wider society' (Macken *et al.*, 1990: Book 1, 6):

Story genres	*Factual genres*
Narrative	Procedure
News story	Explanation
Exemplum	Report
Anecdote	Exposition
Recount	Discussion

This is certainly a range beyond simple storytelling, but we note that no rationale is given for choosing these genres' rather than others which may be equally important. If there is a system behind the choice, it is not spelt out for teachers. On the face of it, this is not a theoretically-based set.

Next, how are the genres defined? Let us take the section on Report as an example (page 4). Like all the others this opens with a general definition of 'Function':

[Report is a] factual text which describes the way things are, with reference to a whole range of phenomena, natural, synthetic and social in our environment.

What about the social purpose of a Report. Is it for reader and writer? What about the participants' goals? What about the context? These key defining properties of Reports are simply omitted. We find it difficult to understand why the theory is not implemented at this point.

The second heading deals with 'Schematic structure'. For 'Report' this reads as follows:

- General classification.
- Description – types;
        – parts (and their functions);
        – qualities;
        – habits/behaviour patterns (or 'uses' if non-natural).

This is, of course, an example of 'staging'. There is nothing wrong with this, but there must be millions of reports of this type which have a different staged structure. Why this structure is selected rather than others is again neither explained nor theoretically justified. Instead of learning to ask what order to put things in, for whom and why [and with what range of response in view], students in years 3–6 are being expected to follow a formula.

In effect, something worse may be happening. We are left thinking that only texts which open with a classification count as reports. In the terms of this manual, anything else is either wrong or is not a report. In other words, this particular schematic structure has become part of a normative definition. Who does that empower, we wonder, apart from the textbook writer?

The final heading is 'Language features'. For 'Report', four distinctive features are listed:

- generic participants [like 'the heart'];
- use of simple present tense;
- no temporal sequence;
- use of 'being' and 'having' clauses.

Again, these appear to be normative. If so, there are some crucial consequences. The heart, it is pointed out, has two hard-working pumps, but in a report on 'The Heart' it will not be permissible to include an account of the way those pumps work. This, of course, could involve 'material (action) clauses' in 'temporal conjunctive relations' (language features that belong to a different genre, in this case Procedures.) Primary school students, it seems, should not learn to blend reports and procedures. Is this the way we use language socially in the real world? Or is it simply another example, alas, of classroom practices cut off from the complexity of real life?

Further directions for practice and theory?

In terms of implementation, then, we see serious dangers arising from the application of the Australian group's work. Yet we, like them, want students to be able to use and control writing for a range of social purposes. We also want to empower students, both within the classroom and – especially – when they move outside it to participate in wider social activities. We know that they will need recurrent encouragement to experiment with and consciously discuss a range of structuring options. We fully realize that there will be both unconscious and conscious modelling on other writers.

The problem manifestly is how to get a purchase on this complex task – and to do so in classrooms where there are many other things going on, either across the curriculum in primary schools or within English at the secondary stage (or in the vocational college).

What can be done? Here are four proposals. First, let us agree that it is not enough to have the four categories of Scottish rhetoric or the range of function categories proposed by the London Writing research – useful though the latter have been.

There is an urgent need to refine the way *all* of us think about writing and reading as purposeful social activities. For example, take the speech act verbs that we quoted from the Cox Report early in this paper: reporting, narrating, persuading, arguing, etc. Useful as they are, we need a better provisional map. The Cox Committee had two domains in mind, 'thinking and learning' and 'communicating meaning to others', but they left some crucial gaps. The biggest is that we want to foster written *dialogue* in the classroom and beyond. That is a major new domain with exciting possibilities.

Take what we have been doing here in this paper: our Australian colleagues have asserted and we have countered. The focus has been on argument, on a speech act family that covers assent and dissent. If we had been face to face with the group, things might have been different: we could all have negotiated instead. In effect, of course, that is what we two have been doing as we jointly wrote this article. We have taken turns to propose the wording, inviting constructive qualifications and even transformations of our first ideas. There has been room for constructive agreement and difference – for speech acts of another family, such as agreeing, differing, etc.

In good classrooms there are many parallels. Commenting on students' drafts, teachers have learnt both to offer a written response and to invite the student to comment in return. Dialogue journals are becoming an important experiment in written form, but there is more going on. In science, groups of students are learning to construct a hypothesis and then to discuss how to test it. In analysing historical documents, they are learning to jot down alternative interpretations and to discuss the problem of selecting which is the more appropriate. The same is happening in reading poetry or in any other text-based study. So our first claim is that a map of 'purposeful social activities' has to include dialogic acts, in speech and writing.

Secondly, we would all like to be able to do more than offer an arbitrary or restricted list of functions for thinking, communication and dialogue. We need a provisional review of the whole field of speech acts covering inner and outer speech.

Thirdly, we all need to know more about 'staged' structures, and how they cue different kinds of shaping for experiences and ideas. The simplest way to represent structures of thinking on the page is by diagrams or layouts. These may take the form of topic webs, flow charts, tree diagrams, networks, tabulations, matrices and so on – each with its own characteristic strengths and limitations. We are not sure that these iconic forms are really well understood, especially in the teaching of English. Thus teachers and students need to discuss when and how to use each of them for appropriate purposes. We have to move beyond brain-storming, making notes, drafting and paragraphing – which we have now learnt something about.

When it comes to planning the 'staging' of an extended text, however, there are inevitable limitations to be borne in mind. If the writer is primarily interested in 'informing' the reader, for example, some preplanned structures will normally be useful. However, they may not be enough. Often, in the course of 'informing' there will be a blend of social purposes, with the writer perhaps 'advising', 'suggesting', 'urging' or 'warning'. Preplanning that focuses on structures of 'information' can exclude all of these other purposeful social activities. In the real world, most text is multi-structured, we would claim, with 'emotive' as well as 'referential' structures.

Moreover, if the writer is primarily interested in setting up a dialogic search or exploration with the reader, the planning of structures *has* to be more piecemeal and provisional. A major goal is to leave room for lateral and divergent thinking, for writing – and reading – as discovery. Thus, the script you are reading at this moment was not totally preplanned. The structure was produced by an incremental series of decisions, stage by stage, you might say – obviously with a very wide range of notes and tacit knowledge competing for entry.

Fourthly, we come to the linguistic cues. Ever since James Moffett talked about the contrast between 'what happened' and 'what happens' (1968) it has been obvious that we teachers ought to be more aware of the sets of options that have fundamental effects on what is written.

There are two complementary ways of talking about such options. One is in terms of 'particularizing', 'typifying' or 'generalizing'. Let us call that the cognitive and affective level: it has been a long-term interest of logic and psychology. The other talks in terms of semantic or grammatical cues, a linguistic interest. So in the case of 'generalizing' we might expect to find recurrent examples of the 'simple present [or unmarked] tense', 'being' and 'having' clauses, the generic use of 'the', and so on, to quote from the genre group's recent list (Christie *et al.*, 1989).

Of course, there are all kinds of other options, which can equally be talked about at either level. Some will have effects well beyond the sentence: think of the range from tentative to assertive, for example, cued by 'perhaps', 'certainly', 'probably' and other modal forms. We need a map of these sets of options, within the sentence and beyond.

There is a big job to be done, then; but the question cannot stop short at naming the choice of options currently being made in class, as the genre theorists seem to be doing. On the contrary, there are choices entrenched in classroom practices which actually work against the kind of teaching and learning we want to foster. [We tried to show this, for example, when we analysed typical questions about poems and literary characters (Dixon and Stratta, 1985, 1986) and showed alternative choices that teachers were already making for the better.]

We are calling, then, for a critical review of the (unconscious) choices already being taken, for better and worse. Where are current generic choices and strategies letting down the learner? What further sets could be incorporated into day-to-day dialogues of the classroom to the learner's benefit? A task on this scale probably calls for an international effort, but, after all, some of us study writing (and society) in order to change it! If this is so, we conclude by asking: Where would be the best place to begin? And who will join in?

9 Defining reading standards: establishing the operational validity of assessments

PAMELA J.K. OWEN

Introduction: a question of standards·

Tolstoy, writing in the latter half of the nineteenth century and disgruntled with contemporary educational practice, observed in one of his Pedagogical Essays:

> Very many people are at the present time very seriously busy finding, borrowing, or inventing the best method for the instruction of reading.
>
> (1862 trans 1967: 32)

His words describe educational practice in the Russia, Europe and America of his time, but seem to be an apt reflection of contemporary concerns about reading standards. It has always proved difficult to determine the best way to teach and assess reading. Tolstoy placed high value on diagnostic assessment undertaken by the teacher, concluding that in reading instruction: 'The best teacher will be he who has at his tongue's end the explanation of what it is that is bothering the pupil' (1862: 58).

Implicit in this comment is the notion that the teacher will not merely be able to diagnose difficulties, but also be able to do something about them. It is not sufficient for teachers simply to record how children are progressing or for examining boards and testing agencies to report levels of competence. To improve standards rather than simply to record and report them, assessment procedures must themselves be accountable. They must provide usable and useful feedback on performance. They must be formative.

It is disheartening to be faced today with the kind of spurious argument that all examinations of learning are useless. Gethin, for example, maintains that it is 'impossible to use exams as a means of comparing language abilities over the years. One is left with nothing but personal impressions to go on. My own is that, if anything, standards have fallen somewhat' (1990: 63). There appears to linger in education a certain kind of 'reflex anti-testing reaction' (Hewlett, 1990) in which external assessment is interpreted as a threat to the professionalism of teachers. Such an attitude stems from experience of having to administer tests which distort the curriculum rather than enhance it. However, the curriculum is not just what is taught and how it is taught. It is also, as George Tolley (1989) points out, the way in which outcomes are assessed. At the time of writing, proposals for adopting a formative criterion-referenced model of assessment hold out the potential for a National Assessment system which is teacher-based and led. However, teacher assessment cannot simply be adopted as an article of faith. If teachers are the agents of improved performance they need an effective procedure for evaluating the effectiveness of instruction. It needs to be demonstrated that an operational framework can be constructed in which teacher-based assessment procedures can be standardized and the assessment data fulfil both summative and formative functions.

The current concern about reading standards seems to stem to a large degree from general uncertainty about the way in which reading achievement can be measured. Back in 1975 the Bullock Committee's Report *A Language for Life* (DES, 1975) concluded that the test materials available at the time were less than adequate in terms of passing judgements upon reading standards. Standardized test materials have changed little in concept since that time and consequently the position of Bullock remains true today.

This has been demonstrated most recently with the results from the 1991 survey into reading test scores conducted by the National Foundation for Educational Research (NFER), where a spokesperson for the agency has pointed out that the unreliability of the normative standardized tests from which data were collected meant there was insufficient evidence to establish the degree or direction of fluctuations in standards.

The complexity of the reading process, disagreement about the most effective methods for teaching reading and the traditional approach to assessment in which test items are selected for their discriminatory rather than their diagnostic power have led to test results which indicate little to the child or to the teacher about specific competences or effective strategies. Past experience shows only too clearly that where test materials are very narrow, they lack validity in comparison with any theoretical or observed model of the reading process although the higher is their test–retest reliability. Thus, word recognition lists and sentence completion tests are highly reliable in test–retest situations, but tell us little about the child's success on a range of everyday reading tasks.

The problem

Aubret and Chartier (1988) in summing up the state of the art with respect to the assessment of reading maintain that 'reading has never been assessed in a satisfactory manner'. In drawing attention to the confusion which exists in reading research about the validity of the various approaches currently being used to test reading competence, they classify approaches to reading assessment into two broad forms: the 'global approach' and the 'analytic evaluation of the basic skills'. Traditional standardized, norm-referenced reading tests and most teacher devised tests are of the global kind. The more recent criterion-referenced reading tests adopt a more analytic approach.

Both approaches have their weaknesses. The global approach, based on standard psychometric methods involving either a straightforward tabulation of the number of correct responses or a ranking of overall performance against a reference population has the weakness of being unable to provide diagnostic information. On the other hand, analytic assessment, which attempts to evaluate reading performance in terms of reading skills or strategies, may provide reliable assessments of sub-skills, but it will not necessarily result in a valid assessment of the reading process as a whole.

The problem is the age-old one of the part/whole dichotomy characterized by Schleiermacher in the eighteenth century as the 'hermeneutic circle'. This he defined as

> the logically vexing proposition that the whole is understood from the parts and the parts from the whole.   (1809/1977: 5)

Current research into reading emphasizes process over product, but views differ about the way in which readers assign meanings to texts. Those who promote a holistic, psycholinguistic approach emphasize the role of hypothesis testing or what Schleiermacher would describe as the 'divinatory' aspect while theorists who embrace a bottom-up approach emphasize word fluency, a feature of Schleiermacher's analytic approach. Recent attempts to mediate between the two by devising an 'interactionist model' of reading have done nothing but obfuscate the issue. The current focus of attention in England at Key Stage One (ages 5–7) has translated the issue quite inappropriately into a debate about the 'whole book' versus the phonic approach.

Schleiermacher's conception of the hermeneutic circle suggests that according priority to one of these approaches over the other in either the teaching or the assessment of reading is a failure to recognize the dialectic of the whole and the parts. If the parts are built up to form the whole, the whole will be no more than the sum of the parts. Equally, if the whole is used merely to direct attention to specific parts then the whole will not even be comprised of the parts. The hermeneutic circle has become a vicious circle in debates about reading.

Teachers are usually well aware of the limitations of their children's reading performance in global terms. However, decisions about the most effective remediation strategies to deploy in particular cases have heretofore been hampered by the lack of a clear definition of the domain or universe which reading circumscribes. Desmond Nuttall has pointed out that 'One is most likely to improve validity by improving the sampling of tasks and contexts from the universe of interest – and that means defining the universe much more carefully than we have done in the past' (1989: 271).

The validity of any form of assessment whether informal or formal is dependent upon the degree to which the criteria on which judgements are based relate to the competences which make up the achievement. This requires a principled language model which can be taught and assessed.

There are thus two problems to be addressed in any attempt to establish and, more importantly, improve standards of reading: one to identify the nature of reading competence and the other to find an approach to assessment which will provide information which can be used formatively, as well as yielding a summative score. Although separate problems, one being to do with the reading process and the other with the assessment process, a single solution can be found for both.

A genre-based solution

Like Aubret and Chartier, few can be satisfied with the validity of existing reading tests. Nevertheless, as Farr et al. note, despite all the problems:

> The assessment of reading performance is a pragmatic, immutable phenomenon in the world of education. Often criticized, reading tests continue nevertheless to be developed, administered, and – theoretical issues not withstanding – believed in.   (1986: 135)

The central problem is, if we are not satisfied with existing tests what do we put in their place?

A major difficulty with traditional approaches to the assessment of reading has been that because of the 'passage dependency' of tests, reading performance on one occasion in relation to one text has not necessarily transferred to performance in relation to another text on another occasion. One possible reason for this is the prevalence of the conceptualization of reading as comprehension. Assessments of comprehension which are designed to measure reading skill typically make one of two basic errors. They either focus on the content or knowledge which the text presents, as in summaries or concept identification tasks, or they draw on a combination of linguistic and cognitive intuitions which might help readers solve textual puzzles, as in cloze tests.

It is worth considering what would result from focusing not on comprehension but on knowledge and understanding in the assessment of reading. Replacing the term 'comprehension' with 'understanding' integrates the whole and the parts in both the teaching and the assessment of reading. Rather than talk about 'top-down' and 'bottom-up approaches' or 'decoding' and 'comprehension', 'real books' or 'phonics', testing or no testing, attention is given to forms of knowledge and the interaction of these in the reading process.

'Understanding' should not, however, be taken to be the appropriation of another's meaning, as was the traditional view in Literary Criticism. This definition stems from the notion that meaning is in some way attached to a text, a view which has been now largely discredited in literary theory as it has in reading theory. An alternative and more promising view is to regard understanding as the extension of a reader's knowledge: understanding which results not from what the text 'represents', but from the 'fusion of horizons' (Gadamer, 1976), which occurs when reader and writer share conventions of coding through their knowledge of genre.

Current practice tends to look at reading from the point of view of what it can achieve, but not from the knowledge of language which it requires. However, to be a formative influence, assessments of reading competence must measure students' understanding of what texts are doing and how they are doing it – an understanding of written texts as communicative objects – rather than confining themselves to an evaluation of comprehension of substantive content matter. This is not to suggest that 'reading for meaning' should be ignored – on the contrary – but the meanings of a text can be many and varied. Only when understanding of the purpose or use of a text and its component parts has been reached and the reading purpose clarified can any sensible meaningful processing take place. It may well be that children often fail to learn from texts precisely because they do not know what the text 'is' as opposed to what it 'says'.

It is universally acknowledged that language proficiency is a function of the context in which communication takes place. It follows that the measurement of reading competence must take account of contexts of communication. Schleiermacher recognized this. He extended the whole/part relationship beyond the individual text to a body of discourse already existing in the reader's experience as a set of conventions which the text presupposes. In so doing he emphasized the importance of rhetorical form, noting that 'The whole is first understood as genre' (Schleiermacher, 1977: 60).

Genres are relatively stable patterns of significance and relate to all forms of purposeful discourse. They arise from particular conventionalized social situations (Kress, 1982) and represent traditional ways of structuring discourse, the instantiation of which can be found in texts of particular types.

There would appear to be little if any evidence to suggest that the principles used for classifying written texts should not be used as descriptors of interpretive possibilities – guidelines to understanding. Learning to read is a process of acquiring knowledge of these guidelines and the appropriate strategies to use in processing specific types of texts in relation to specific reading purposes. Judd and Buswell (1922) demonstrated almost seventy years ago that reading purpose and type of reading material affect readers' processing of text. This finding has been supported by numerous studies since and acknowledged in large scale surveys of reading performance. For example, in the reading surveys conducted by the Assessment of Performance

Unit and the Scottish Language Monitoring Project (see Neville, 1988), pupils were presented with reading passages of different genre forms – expository, narrative and functional – and asked questions which, it was stated, varied 'according to the type of material being read' (DES, 1983: 4).

More recently the Kingman (DES, 1988b) and Cox (DES, 1988a) Reports have underlined the importance of genre, advocating that 'children should read an increasingly wide range and variety of texts' and 'should be shown how to read different kinds of materials in different ways' (1988a: 30/31).

However, despite the fact that there is considerable information available about the generic structure of texts and the importance of genre expectations in shaping reader behaviour, the importance of the concept of genre in the teaching and assessment of reading, although undoubtedly well established, is not exploited to its full extent. In an interview reported in *The English Magazine* Gunther Kress expressed his concern about this. He stated that knowledge about genres 'is not being made explicitly available when it should be, and is therefore, being transmitted by osmosis' (1991: 5).

Assessments of reading must judge a pupil's interpretive skills by reference to the rhetorical form of the text or texts to allow for the generalizability of questions and responses across passages of the same generic form, and to enable feedback to relate directly to reading procedures rather than to substantive content.

Describing stages of progression

The National Curriculum for England and Wales provides a model of the reading process which can be accepted as the basis of the construct and content validity of any assessment materials produced to monitor performance within it. National Assessment assumes levels of competence; progression assumes developmental stages; the curriculum assumes a relationship between the two which is formative.

It is here that the potential of the genre-based approach can be realized. In the National Curriculum the Statements of Attainment (SoA) for Reading serve the purpose well. In strands they combine to link the three elements of the assessment triad. They

● represent domains of knowledge;
● characterize reading material;
● describe levels of achievement.

However, related SoA at different levels are often vaguely expressed. The teacher is left with the task of deciding what precise elements of growth are demanded from one level to another. For example, in EN2 (Reading), SoA 3a asks that the pupil 'read aloud from familiar stories and poems fluently and with appropriate expression', while SoA 4a asks that the pupil 'read aloud expressively, fluently and with increased confidence from a range of familiar literature'. There is little indication either within or between these

SoA of the growth which would be demanded at Level 4 as against that to be achieved at Level 3.

Hereby enters an issue embedded within the entire debate about reading standards, that of how to differentiate levels of achievement. There are two main approaches which can be taken. In the first, differentiation by outcome, a common task is designed and performance levels are established by reference to the quality of the response. In the second, a variety of levelled tasks is set and matched to an individual child's stage of development. In the first case all children start and finish at the same point. In the second case the teacher determines the appropriate entry and exit point for each child.

Should levels of performance be judged by grading tasks or evaluating responses? Experience from the National Pilot tests at Key Stage 1 (age 7) suggests the former. The use of a common assessment task means that the single task is inevitably pitched at too high a level for some children and too low a level for others. Children cannot demonstrate their achievements in such circumstances. A Schools Examinations and Assessment Council officer commented after the national pilot tests, 'Lower attaining pupils were found in the pilot to benefit from tasks well matched to their capabilities. Higher attaining pupils were disadvantaged by tasks at too low a level.' This surely must represent no more than the knowledge all teachers have of teaching children at different stages of development.

If a child's reading competence is to be judged in procedural rather than relative terms then assessment must discriminate between tasks not children. It is tasks which need to be graded not children. There is no such thing as a Level 2 child. Children demonstrate jagged profiles of attainment. There are, however, Level 2 tasks. The consequences of performance must be provided by the task itself and the criteria of success made explicit and fully attainable. Otherwise, pupils are caught in a no-win situation in which their performance is always seen to be deficient in some way. The following comment by Pumfrey is a clear illustration of an assumption that testing is all about labelling children and separating them into groups as good, average or poor.

> Even if all 7 year old children in Britain could accurately, fluently and with comprehension read Shakespeare, some would do so more accurately, fluently and with greater comprehension than others.   (Pumfrey, 1990)

In order to define reading standards in terms of an individual child's stage of progression, a way has to be found to grade reading tasks by reference to text types, text levels, reading purposes. All three demand genre-based criteria of an appropriate response.

Teachers' use of genre

There are four main genre forms described in the National Curriculum: narraative; non-narrative; 'real life'; and poetry. Few would disagree that

Table 9.1   Judging the type

Type	% Agreed	Confused with
Narrative		
traditional	74	other narrative
real life	73	fantasy narrative
fantasy	81	real life narrative
anthologies	93	
Non-narrative		
reference	94	
instructional	92	topic-specific
topic-specific	98	
Real life		
classroom info	–	
public info	67	real life narrative
periodicals/comics	–	
Poetry		
poetry/drama	72	narrative
word games	100	anthologies

reading competence needs to be judged in relation to all of them. What are the chances that it will be? Early indications from a project involving 45 primary and middle school teachers in a northern LEA suggest that there is a strong element of agreement in attempts to specify type of reading material drawn from the classrooms of children in Years 1–6.

The teachers were asked to identify the four genres of classroom text and to arrive at a consensus through group discussion. They then independently classified sixty-four texts of ten types, with three independent readers for each text. (The results are shown in Table 9.1.)

The chance level of agreement would be 9 per cent. Ninety per cent agreement is the norm. Teachers, as one would expect of experienced readers, have a powerful intuitive sense of genre.

Teachers were then asked to do a survey of their own text holdings (see Table 9.2).

The emphasis on narrative text and the under-representation of poetry suggest that children are not getting a wide range of reading experience. Moreover, there is no real evidence of any trend towards a different kind of reading material as the child gets older. Any progression is within these genres, not across them.

The genres in themselves therefore do not deal with the notion of 'readability'. The problems with traditional readability measures have been well documented. All essentially relate to the fact that they predict text difficulty

Table 9.2   Text holdings: 27 teachers, at least three per year group

Year	% Narrative	% Non-narrative	% Real life	% Poetry	Average number of books
1	47	33	11	9	343
2	51	28	12	9	379
3	50	38	3	8	249
4	48	39	8	5	380
5	60	31	6	3	563
6	44	50	0	3	384

Table 9.3   Judging the level (292 pairs, 67 per cent agree on level)

Judgements involving	Two down	One down	Agreed	One up	Two up
Level 1	–	–	28%	67%	5%
Level 2	–	32%	56%	12%	
Level 3	2%	8%	74%	16%	
Level 4		23%	64%	13%	–
Level 5		30%	70%	–	–

rather than describe sources of text difficulty. This has led some researchers, Perera (1980) for example, to suggest informed subjective judgement as an alternative.

> Informed judgements by a thoughtful teacher may have advantages over the application of a readability formula.   (1980: 151)

In a further session teachers were asked to judge the level of text, 'level' referring to the National Curriculum reading Levels 1–10. There was a 77 per cent agreement between pairs of teachers judging text independently (Table 9.3).

Only the concept of a Level 1 text caused real disagreement, which was not surprising in view of the National Curriculum's definition of Level 1 reading: few texts require children to differentiate between letters and numbers. This subjective classification was again applied to the teachers' holdings (Table 9.4). On the National Curriculum scale, one point equates to two years of average reading progress.

The disadvantages of informed subjective judgements are manifest, unless mastery of the reading process is complete by Year 4 (ages 8–9). As long as the criteria of genre difficulty remain implicit they cannot be highlighted in

Table 9.4   Levels of narrative text by year group taught

	(1) %	(2) %	(3) %	(4) %	(5) %	Number of books	Mean level
Infant (Y1 + Y2)	30	43	24	2	0	2470	1.9
Junior (Y3 + Y4)	2	24	29	27	18	1310	3.4
Junior (Y5 + Y6)	4	22	27	27	20	2315	3.4

programmes of study as features to draw to the attention of children when reading different types of texts. What is required is some measure which is not only predictive, but also diagnostic – a measure which indicates what factors cause the reader to have difficulty with a text.

There are many complexities in language which affect the difficulty of a reading text and it is likely that a single metric of complexity would be difficult to achieve. The processing load of a text is predicted not only by intuitive response to the different manifestations of different dimensions of discourse, but by analysis of the structuring of information at different 'levels' of text.

A number of theorists have drawn attention to text levels when attempting to describe the appropriateness of reading strategies in relation to a particular text. Curtis and Glaser refer to reading as 'a process in which information from several levels must be combined' (1983). They specify word decoding; word meaning; sentence processing; discourse analysis. Fredrikson (1981) focuses on two of these, word analysis processes and discourse analysis processes, and maintains that a reader draws on knowledge from two bases – orthographic and semantic – to integrate the two. Sanford and Garrod refer to 'comprehension at all levels – words, sentences and complete tracts of discourse' (1981: 3). McClelland writes, 'When we process language – either in written or in spoken form – we construct representations of what we are processing at many different levels' (1987: 3) and specifies letter, word, sentence and larger units of text.

Broadly speaking, this suggests that to interpret written language appropriately requires readers to have knowledge of the manifestation of the communicative strategies used by writers at four 'levels' of analysis: global, local, sentence and word. Textual characteristics at these levels also provide a means of describing the difficulty level of a text. Informal observation of junior school teachers at work suggests that they rarely intervene at other than the word or sentence level. However, following the traditional methodology of the hermeneutic circle the emphasis in reading assessment must be on the whole communicative process and the language routines of which it is comprised rather than on the routines alone, with the expectation that an aggregrate of the parts will in some way represent the whole. It is an appreciation of the developing complexity at the global level which is missing. Is it possible to begin to analyse the developing features of genre?

A genre classification

The question is, what is it about each class type which is distinctive and how can the generic characteristics of each be captured within a framework for learning? Rhetoricians, both ancient and modern, have tended to differentiate discourse, both spoken and written on two bases: purpose and audience. In contrast, linguists have in the main used structural divisions to differentiate between different types of writing. When these principles are combined to classify discourse they form a three-parameter framework for describing the defining characteristics of genre form.

The **audience** parameter reflects the relationship between the reader and writer, with variation according to whether the focus of the writing is placed on the reader, writer or subject matter (Kinneavy, 1971). The second parameter, **purpose**, reflects the way in which the writer deploys information with variation in terms of what Wilkinson and others have defined as describing, generalizing and speculating. This dimension features in a number of alternative models being variously called 'aims' (Kinneavey, 1971), 'function' (Jakobson, 1960; Britton *et al.*, 1975), 'force' (Brewer, 1980), 'forms' (Moffett, 1968). **Organization**, the third parameter, differentiates discourse in terms of the sequencing principles used to order information. The three basic forms of connection or organization – temporal, topical and logical – have been referred to by Wilkinson as 'primary acts of mind' (1986: 128) and are widely supported by many other theorists (Brewer, 1980; Kress, 1982; Longacre, 1983).

These nine generic traits represented in Table 9.5 provide cues to readers as they endeavour to understand and recall textual information.

The three dimensions in Table 9.5 provide a structure for demonstrating how the learner develops knowledge of language use within the specified contexts of communication represented by genres. For example, expository

Table 9.5   Generic traits

Audience	Purpose	Organization
writer	describe	temporal
subject	generalize	topical
reader	speculate	logical

text is characterized by a focus on the **subject** matter, with information used to **generalize** and is structured by aspects of the **topic**. Narrative text, by way of contrast, is characterized by a focus on the **reader**, with the same use of information to **generalize**, but this time structured according to a **temporal** principle.

Progression within a genre can also be identified. Three different forms of argument can be used to illustrate this. Sophisticated argument will focus on the **reader**, use information to **speculate** and use a **logical** form of organization. An elementary form of argument such as personal viewpoint has a 'writer + describe + topical' profile. A more advanced form such as personal opinion features the same **writer** focus and **topical** form of organization as the elementary form, but here information is used to **generalize**.

To understand what a text 'is' there are three sources of evidence: a general impression of the rhetorical orientation of the writing as established by schematic predictions of genre form; specific features at the global and local levels of text; and grammatical and orthographic characteristics. No one source is of itself a sufficient route to 'understanding' the whole. As Reilley, in an explication of his control processing model of reading has commented, 'All sources of information are focused on the task of analysing the input at any given time' (1985: 16).

Conclusion

Carr and Kemmis (1983) list five formal requirements for any adequate and coherent method of investigation into and improvement of educational standards:

1 A rejection of positivistic notions such as absolute standards.
2 Use of the interpretive categories of teachers.
3 Identification of distortions by ideology.
4 The exposure of elements in the existing system which frustrate change.
5 Confidence in the practicability of the measures.

These seem to be a valuable set of guidelines when attempting to put into place teacher-based assessments of reading. This paper has attempted to describe requirement 4, one of whose elements is the inadequacy of requirement 2. It must be left to others, however, to judge whether strengthening requirement 2 runs the danger of introducing further distortions by ideology.

A reading curriculum based on the notion of genre serves as a heuristic for both teacher and pupil to identify the child's progress in learning how to communicate within the universe of discourse. Defining reading standards using teacher assessments puts control in the hands of practitioners, but it also demands their accountability. All educationalists are accountable and there is a responsibility on all to provide teachers with a more acute analysis of what genre entails and an understanding that progression within genre is the only worthwhile focus for any concern at all about defining 'standards'.

This paper has set out to present a view of reading assessment which is teacher controlled, theoretically principled, standardized, but flexible – a view which seeks to ensure the operational validity of the process and thus meet the needs of the individual child.

10 Experience versus instruction: the continuing dilemma

JAMES R. SQUIRE

For the greater part of this century, our schools, at least American schools, have been unable to achieve an equilibrium involving both instruction and learning – a balance between the extent to which we should interfere with natural processes of language acquisition and language learning to present appropriate instruction, and the extent to which we need only establish a print-rich, literate learning environment, and let children and young people develop competence on their own.

Those who opt for a rich language activity see the schools' task as one which focuses on guidance of natural learning. They tend to rely on that aspect of Vygotsky's work which stresses learning in social context, forgetting Vygotsky's deep interest in cognitive challenge (1965). They are convinced that children will develop competence in the uses of language as they read, write and talk in ever more complex meaning-making activity.

Those who opt for instruction see the teacher's role as central. They feel that the only sure way to guarantee that all children will read, write and talk at reasonable levels is to teach the fundamental skills and processes, and then provide opportunity for children to practice.

The controversy first exploded in America during the heyday of American progressive education when an activity-centred language arts curriculum became the order of the day. The great philosopher, John Dewey, provided the instructional model; but too many progressive educators failed to heed Dewey's warning that an activity becomes a real learning experience only when an individual *thinks* about what has occurred. The learning then comes not from the doing, but from thinking about the doing, whether by writing or talking. Interactive language classrooms with lots of attention to analysing the activities thus became the norm – some forty to fifty years before resurfacing in Jimmy Britton's great book, *Language and Learning* (1970), obviously influenced in part even if indirectly by the theories of John Dewey.

In the 1940s and 1950s American schools moved to an emphasis on presentation and teaching. Indeed, one central issue of that time was determining which elements of grammar should be taught. Or what forms of English usage should receive emphasis. Or which should receive no emphasis. Or the ultimate question prior to the 1967 Dartmouth Seminar: What is English? What is the content that we teach?

The conflict of teaching and experience emerged again in the 1960s when child-centred models of language learning appeared in the British infant schools of the day, from ideas advanced at the Dartmouth Seminar, and from liberal American language thinkers like Jim Moffett (although admittedly Moffett never abandoned his belief that classroom freedom of activity could be achieved only when set against a rather rigorous, disciplined control underlying expanded uses of language).

Then the urban revolution in American schools and the influx of large numbers of new Americans who spoke little or no English led to an awareness of severe inadequacies in learning and teaching in our central city schools and ultimately to development of the mastery learning approach – the work of Benjamin Bloom, Madeline Hunter and Ethna Reid, among others – stressing teaching and drilling on the specific skills of reading and writing. Dozens of studies of effective teaching and effective schooling in American slum schools identified desirable practices – direct instruction, time on task, the teach-test-and-reteach cycle, and so forth. Clearly, the portrait of good teaching in these studies of the seventies was of the teacher at the podium instructing the class. The amount of teaching time, indeed, was identified as a key variable in defining effective teaching. Our tests of reading and writing competence, all based on mastery of specific skills, documented each achievement of such schools. For a time, skill-orientated instruction dominated American education.

What moved teachers and schools again toward student-centred experience were our new insights into the writing process – and subsequently the reading process – which emerged in the late 1970s and were propounded through the summer writing projects of Jim Gray and company at the University of California at Berkeley, aided and abetted by recommendations from the London Institute of Education (Jimmy Britton, Nancy Martin, Harold Rosen and others) as well as Don Graves' Writing to Reading Center in New Hampshire, the Iowa Writing Workshops, and the Bread Loaf Writing Institute. The fact that a single publisher, Robert Boynton (now part of America's Heinemann) rose to prominence publishing book after book on student-centred writing (Graves, Culkin, Atwell, Newkirk, as well as imported titles), aided and abetted the communication of ideas concerning student-centred process. Because of widespread dissatisfaction with skill-centred 'Back to Basics', the interest in process inherited from cognitive psychology and increasingly applied to reading as well as writing, and the stimulation from Louise Rosenblatt's book on response to reading – *The Reader, the Text, the Poem* (1978) – the interest of American teachers again shifted away from telling, teaching, and testing 'to student-centred language activity, to the processes of writing, reading, and thinking.'

The widespread 'whole language' effort to relate talk, writing and reading in integrated 'meaning-making' activities in the classroom is clearly part of this development in America, although it has been strongly influenced by school practices in New Zealand and Australia. Strongest at the primary level where it represents a shift away from skill-orientated mastery programmes and from those basal reading programmes which stress skill development, 'whole language' is a major trend in American and Canadian schools, presently generating a new research agenda since, except for some case studies and ethnographic analyses, most of today's practices in America are not research-based. Curiously, practitioners look to Vygotsky and Piaget as forerunners, seldom to Dewey (who almost certainly influenced the more recent theorists).

Worth noting is that in the USA the strength of 'whole language' resides in suburban and rural schools, not in urban settings where skill teaching remains in the forefront of much teaching. Administrators of our tough urban schools, desperate to report even the beginnings of literacy, are not overly impressed with talk of print-rich environments and 'meaning-making' activities. Worth noting, also, is the strong increase in wide reading by children of books now being promoted in 'whole language' programmes, even though the most influential impetus for such wide reading came from the Center for the Study of Reading, which found that many skill-orientated programmes allowed little time for reading. Schools were too busy telling, teaching and testing lists of discrete skills. This, from an influential centre of research in skill development.

Thus, today, American schools face again the dilemma of the 1930s, 1960s and 1970s. How much language activity? How much instruction?

There is much to commend in today's integrated programme – wide reading of books, for instance, accompanied by sharing; extensive writing and publishing of writing; excited talk; even better books and increased time for more kinds of language activity.

However, the evidence becomes increasingly clear that, however exciting many of these programmes are, they could be made even stronger with the addition of an instructional component. Were there no need for helping students to learn, there would be no need for professional teaching. We really could revert to 'shopping mall schools', filled with books, word processors, places to talk and think, but not with teachers. Children could be locked into these schools every morning and we could trust that something worthwhile would happen during the day.

Small chance. Everything I know from research of many kinds indicates that only the linguistically-able children will really learn on their own from a rich diet of literary activities; perhaps 15 per cent of our students. The others, I would guess from 80 to 85 per cent of our children, will profit, often profit extensively, from some instructional activity. What else is the influential Reading Recovery programme of Marie Clay – so popular in New Zealand and now the USA – but a highly structured intervention to help young children learn to read.

However, instruction need not be directed only from the dais – as Frank Whitehead long since has pointed out. *Direct instruction* with either mini-lectures or maxi-, is only one way of teaching children.

Conferencing, whether with one or more children, offers an important alternative – and one much admired by Donald Graves and many composing specialists, as a way of providing help within the context of the writing process when the learner most needs such help.

Guiding or *nudging* by the teacher offers yet another strategy which 'soft-pedals' the instructional component. (I recall watching small children hammer and pound endlessly in a British infant school 23 years ago, and asking one Headmistress what she did if the children kept hammering and pounding, and never got ready for reading. 'Why, sir,' she said incredu-lously, 'I just nudge them a little.' And so she did. And so they moved.)

Peer tutoring as well as *teacher tutoring* offers yet other approaches to providing instruction. So does *scaffolding* through which we try to construct classroom support activity to ensure that certain kinds of learning seem almost inevitable. *Modelling* is important, too, especially modelling text structures to guide subsequent reading and writing. The more so if boys and girls can be made aware of what we are doing, and why they are writing and reading certain kinds of texts.

Collaborative learning of any kind, most particularly the variant called *co-operative learning* in American schools, where students engage in thinking through concepts together and the activity itself provides yet another way of providing instruction. Here particularly, I think we need to focus with our students on what is being learned co-operatively and on what learning theories may be involved.

Reciprocal teaching, Ann Palinscar and Ann Brown's strategies for involv-ing teachers and students in oral language exchanges, seems to me a structured variant on other kinds of co-operative learning. However, it surely provides for carefully planned instruction, however indirectly it is presented.

All of these, and no doubt many other strategies, can help us provide an instructional component within meaning-orientated teaching programmes. I have tried to emphasize that almost all children need some kind of instruc-tion, even within meaning-orientated teaching; but that there are many ways to deliver such necessary instruction. I see no reason why instruction and learning activities should be considered incompatible. Rather, I would argue that the two are mutually supportive. As Britton and Charney (in Flood *et al.*, 1991) have recently written:

Teachers structure learning situations within which students talk, write, read and listen under the guidance of the teacher/expert. The teacher is alert to the students' use of specific curriculum skills and processes, mentally ticking the curriculum items off, as it were, and assessing the proficiency in the course of ongoing work.

I would add, providing within the context of the ongoing work whatever instruction each individual requires.

References

Achebe, C. (1988) 'Arrow of God'. In *The African Trilogy*. London, Picador.

Adamson, S. (1990) 'The what of the language'. In C. Ricks and L. Michaels (eds) *The State of the Language*. London, Faber.

Agar, M.H. (1987) 'Political talk: thematic analysis of a policy argument'. In L. Kedar (ed.) *Power Through Discourse*. Norwood, NJ, Ablex, pp. 113–38.

Althusser, L. (1970) 'Ideology and ideological state apparatuses'. In L. Althusser (ed.) *Essays on Ideology* (1971). Great Britain, Verso.

Ardley, N. (1989) *How We Build Oil Rigs*. London, Macmillan.

Arnold, H. (1990) *A Book About Bubbles. Reading for Learning Level One*. London, Macmillan.

Aubret, J. and Chartier, D. (1988) *Reading Assessment and Illetrisme*. Paper presented to the European Conference on Assessment, University of Birmingham, 23 October.

Austin, J.L. (1962) *How to Do Things with Words*. Oxford, Oxford University Press.

Barthes, R. (1973) *Mythologies*, translated by A. Lavers. London, Granada.

Bateman, T.S. and Zeithaml, C.P. (1989) 'The psychological context of strategic decisions: a model and convergent experimental findings'. *Strategic Management Journal*, 10, 59–74.

Becker, T.E. and Klimoski, R.J. (1989) 'A field study of the relationship between the organizational feedback environment and performance'. *Personnel Psychology*, 42, 343–59.

Bell, R. (1988) 'After the takeover: how to read the handwriting on the wall'. In *Management Review*, September 22–9.

Belsey, C. (1980) *Critical Practice*. London, Methuen.

Benton, R. (1985) *Bilingual Education Programmes Evaluation Project* (Final Report). Wellington, NZCER.

Bleich, D. (1978) *Subjective Criticism*. Baltimore, Johns Hopkins University Press.

Bleich, D. (1986) 'Intersubjective readings'. *New Literary History*, 27, 401–21.

Bloom, A. (1987) *The Closing of the American Mind*. New York, Simon and Schuster.

Board of Education (1921) *The Teaching of English in England* (The Newbolt Report). London, HMSO.

Bogdan, D. (1989) 'Romancing the response: issues of engagement and detachment in reading literature'. In P. Artiss, J. Chadwick, A. Hall and J. Snow (eds) *Values and Evaluation: Proceedings of Inkshed V*. St. John's, Newfoundland, Memorial University of Newfoundland, pp. 104–14.

Bogdan, D. and Straw, S. (eds) (1990) *Beyond Communication*. Portsmouth, NH, Boynton/Cook.

Bogdan, D. and Yeomans, S. (1986) 'School censorship and learning values through literature'. *The Journal of Moral Education*, 15(3), 197–211.

Bower, J.L. (1970) *Managing the Resource Allocation Process*. Cambridge, Mass., Harvard University Press.

Brennan, J. and Keaney, L. (1988) *Zoo Day*. London, Dent.

Brewer, W.F. (1980) 'Literary theory, rhetoric and stylistics: implications for psychology'. In R.J. Spiro *et al.* (eds) *Theoretical Issues in Reading Comprehension*. New Jersey, Lawrence Erlbaum.

Britton, J. (1970) *Language and Learning*. Harmondsworth, Penguin.

Britton, J. (1971) 'What's the use? A schematic account of language functions'. *Educational Review*. 23(3), 205–20.

Britton, J., Burgess, T., Martin, N., McLeod, A. and Rosen, H. (1975) *The Development of Writing Abilities 11–18*. London, Macmillan.

Carr, W. and Kemmis, S. (1983) *Becoming Critical: Knowing through Action Research*. Victoria, Deakin University Press.

Carter, C., Nitert, R. and Ritchie, I. (1990) *Air*. Australia, Macmillan.

Carter, E.E. (1971) 'The behavioral theory of the firm and top level corporate decisions'. *Administrative Science Quarterly*, 16, 413–28.

Chall, J.S., Jacobs, V.A. and Baldwin, L.E. (1990) *The Reading Crisis. Why Poor Children Fall Behind*. Cambridge, Mass., Harvard University Press.

Chandler, A.D. (1962) *Strategy and Structure: Chapters in the History of the American Industrial Enterprise*. Cambridge, Mass., M.I. Press.

Chapman, L.J. (1987) *Reading: From 5 to 11 Years*. Milton Keynes, Open University Press.

Christie, F. and Rothery, J. (1989) 'Genres and writing: a response to Michael Rosen'. In *English in Australia*, 90, AATE, pp. 3–12.

Christie, F. and Rothery, J. (1990) 'Literacy in the curriculum: planning and assessment'. In F. Christie (ed.) *Literacy for a Changing World*, Australia Council for Educational Research. England, NFER.

Christie, F. *et al.* (1984) *Language Studies: Children Writing*. Victoria, Deakin University.

Christie, F., Martin, J. and Rothery, J. (1989) 'Genres make meaning'. In *English in Australia*, 90 AATE, 43–59.

Clark, R., Fairclough, N., Ivanic, R. and Martin-Jones, M. (1987) *Critical Language Awareness. Working Paper Series 1*. Centre for Language in Social Life, Lancaster, University of Lancaster.

Commonwealth Government of Australia (1988) *Higher Education: A Policy Statement*. Australia, Canberra.

Connolly, P. (1986) *The Legend of Odysseus*. Oxford, Oxford University Press.

Cox, B. (1991) *Cox on Cox. An English Curriculum for the 1990s*. London, Hodder and Stoughton.

Culler, J. (1982) *On Deconstruction: Theory and Criticism after Structuralism.* Ithaca, NY, Cornell University Press.

Cummins, J. (1984) *Bilingualism and Special Education: Issues in Assessment and Pedagogy.* Clevedon, Avon, Multilingual Matters.

Cummins, J. and Swain, M. (1986) *Bilingualism in Education.* London, Longman.

Curtis, M.E. and Glaser, R. (1983) 'Reading theory and the assessment of reading achievement'. *Journal of Educational Measurement*, 20, 2.

Cutting, B. and Cutting, J. (1988) *The Tree.* London, Sunshine Books, Heinemann Educational.

DES (1975) *A Language for Life* (The Bullock Report). London, HMSO.

DES (1983) 'Language performance in schools', *APU Secondary Survey Report No. 2.* London, HMSO.

DES (1985) *Education for All* (The Swann Report). London, HMSO.

DES (1988a) *English for Ages 5 to 11* (The Cox Report). London, HMSO.

DES (1988b) *Report of the Committee of Enquiry into the Teaching of English* (The Kingman Report). London, HMSO.

DES (1989) *English for Ages 5–16.* London, HMSO.

DES (1990) *The Teaching and Learning of Reading in Primary Schools. A Report by HMI.* London, HMSO.

Dias, P. (1987) *Making Sense of Poetry: Patterns in the Process.* Ottawa, Canadian Council of Teachers of English.

Dick, J. (1982) *Not in Our Schools?!!! School Book Censorship in Canada: A Discussion Guide.* Ottawa, Canadian Library Association.

Dixon, J. (1967) *Growth through English.* Reading, England, National Association for the Teaching of English.

Dixon, J. (1979) *Education for 16–19: The Role of English and Communication.* London, Macmillan Education.

Dixon, J. and Stratta, L. (1985) *Character Studies – Changing the Question.* Sheffield, National Association for the Teaching of English.

Dixon, J. and Stratta, L. (1986) *Examining Poetry – the Need for Change.* Sheffield, The National Association for the Teaching of English.

Dombey, H. (1987) 'What's the use of English? Powerful stuff'. *The Times Educational Supplement*, 1 May.

Donaldson, M. (1989) *Sense and Sensibility, Some Thoughts on the Teaching of Literacy*, Occasional Paper No. 3. Reading, University of Reading.

Dorian, N.C. (1978) 'The dying dialect and the role of the schools'. In J. Alatis (ed.) *International Dimensions of Bilingual Education.* Washington, DC, Georgetown University Press, 646–56.

Edelman, M. (1984) 'The political language of the helping professions'. In M. Shapiro (ed.) *Language and Politics.* Oxford, Basil Blackwell, pp. 44–60.

Eggins, S., Martin, J.R. and Wignell, P. (1987) *Writing Project: Working Papers in Linguistics No. 5.* Sydney, University of Sydney.

Elliott, J. (1989). *The Waterhole.* London, Sunshine Books.

Fairclough, N. (1989) *Language and Power.* New York, Longman.

Farr, R. *et al.* (1986) 'Recent theory and research into the reading process. Implications for reading assessment'. In J. Orasanu (ed.) *Reading Comprehension from Research to Practice.* Hillsdale, Lawrence Erlbaum.

Fetterly, J. (1978) *The Resisting Reader: A Feminist Approach to American Fiction.* Bloomington, IN, Indiana University Press.

Fish, S. (1970) 'Literature in the reader: affective stylistics'. *New Literary History*, 2, 123–62.

Fish, S. (1980) *Is there a Text in this Class? The Authority of Interpretative Communities.* Cambridge, MA, Harvard University Press.

Flood, J., Jensen, J., Lapp, D. and Squire, J.R. (eds) (1991) *Handbook of Research on Teaching the English Language Arts.* New York, Macmillan.

Frederickson, J.W. (1984) 'The comprehensiveness of strategic decision processes: extension, observations, future directions'. *Academy of Management Journal*, 27 (3), 445–66.

Fredrikson, R. (1981) 'Sources of process interactions in reading'. In A.M. Lesgold and C.A. Perfetti *Interactive Processes in Reading.* Hillsdale, Lawrence Erlbaum.

Freire, P. (1960) *Education for Critical Consciousness.* New York, Continuum.

Frye, N. (1971) *The Critical Path: An Essay on the Social Context of Literary Criticism.* Bloomington, Indiana University Press.

Fulford, R. (1989) *Literature and Literacy: The Future of English Studies*, Jackson Lecture 1989. Toronto, Ontario Institute for Studies in Education.

Fussell, P. (1975) *The Great War and Modern Memory.* New York, Oxford University Press.

Gadamer, H.G. (1976) *Philosophical Hermeneutics*, translated and edited by D.E. Linge. Berkeley, University of California Press.

Gee, J.P. (1991) 'Orality and literacy: From *The Savage Mind* to *Ways With Words*'. In V. Lee (ed.) *Children's Learning in School.* London, Hodder & Stoughton.

Gethin, A. (1990) *Antilinguistics: A Critical Assessment of Modern Linguistic Theory and Practice.* Oxford, Intellect.

Giroux, H.A. (1983) *Theory and Resistance in Education: A Pedagogy for the Opposition.* London, Heinemann Educational.

Golding, W. (1954) *Lord of the Flies.* London, Faber.

Graham-Cameron, E. (1977) *The Cambridge Scene.* Cambridge, Dinosaur.

Gramsci, A. (1971) 'Notebooks'. In Q. Hoare and G.N. Smith (eds) *Selection from the Prison Notebooks of Antonio Gramsci.* London, Lawrence and Wishart.

Griffiths, V. (1990) 'Information Book Awards'. *Times Educational Supplement*, 9 November.

Grosjean, F. (1982) *Life with Two Languages. An Introduction to Bilingualism.* Cambridge, Mass., Harvard University Press.

Habermas, J. (1984) *Theory of Communicative Action Vol. 1: Reasoning and the Rationalization of Society*, translated by T. McCarthy. London, Heinemann.

Hakuta, K. (1986) *The Mirror of Language: The Debate on Bilingualism.* New York, Basic Books.

Hall, S. (1980) 'Encoding/Decoding'. In Central Cultural Studies Unit *Culture, Media, Language.* London, Hutchinson.

Halliday, M.A.K. (1985) *Functional Grammar.* London, Edward Arnold.

Halliday, M.A.K. and Hasan, R. (1989) *Language, Context, and Text: Aspects of Language in a Social-semiotic Perspective.* Oxford, Oxford University Press.

Hamers, J. and Blanc, M. (1989) *Bilinguality and Bilingualism.* Cambridge, Cambridge University Press.

Hartman, G. (1980) *Criticism in the Wilderness*. New Haven and London, Yale University Press.

Harvey, D. (1989) *The Condition of Postmodernity*. Oxford, Blackwell.

Hasan, R. (1978) 'Text in the systemic-functional model'. In W.V. Dressler (ed.) *Current Trends in Textlinguistics*. Berlin, de Gruyter.

Hewlett, M. (1990) 'Fitting the National Curriculum to one's own principles'. In T. Brighouse and B. Moon (eds) *Managing the National Curriculum: Some Critical Perspectives*. Harlow, Longman.

Hirsch, E.D., Jr (1987) *Cultural Literacy: What Every American Needs to Know*. Boston, Houghton Mifflin.

Isaacs, E. (1976) *Greek Children in Sydney*. Canberra, Australian National University Press.

Iser, W. (1978) *The Act of Reading: A Theory of Aesthetic Response*. Baltimore, Johns Hopkins University Press.

Iser, W. (1980) 'Texts and readers'. *Discourse Processes*, 3, 327–43.

Ishiguro, K. (1989) *The Remains of the Day*. London, Faber.

Jackall, R. (1983) 'Moral mazes: bureaucracy and managerial work'. *Harvard Business Review*, September–October, 118–29.

Jakobson, R. (1960) 'Linguistics and poetics'. In T.A. Sebeok (ed.) *Style in Language*. New York, John Wiley and Sons.

Janks, H. (1988) 'To Catch a Wake-up: Language Awareness in the South African Context'. University of the Witwatersrand, unpublished MA dissertation.

Janks, H. (1990) 'Contested terrain: English education in South Africa 1948–1987'. In I. Goodson and P. Medway (eds) *Bringing English to Order. The History and Politics of a School Subject*. Lewes, Falmer Press.

Janks, H. (in press) *Language and Position* (Language Matters Series). University of Witwatersrand Press.

Jennings, J. (1989) *Into Science*. Oxford, Oxford University Press.

Jones, D. (1937) *In Parenthesis*. London, Faber.

Judd, C.H. and Buswell, G.T. (1922) *Silent Reading: A Study of the Various Types*, Supplementary Reading Monographs 23. Chicago, University of Chicago Press.

Junction Avenue Theatre Company (1987) 'Tooth and Nail'. Unpublished manuscript.

Kalantzis, M., Cope, W. and Slade, D. (1989) *Minority Languages and Dominant Culture*. Lewes, Falmer Press.

Kedar, L. (ed.) (1987) *Power Through Discourse*. Norwood, NJ, Ablex.

Kemmis, S. (1988) 'Action research'. In J.P. Keeves (ed.) *Educational Research, Methodology, and Measurement: An International Handbook*. Oxford, Pergamon Press.

Kermode, F. (1989) *An Appetite for Poetry*. London, Collins.

Kinneavy, J.L. (1971) *A Theory of Discourse*. Englewood Cliffs, NJ, Prentice Hall.

Kovach, B. (1989) *The Organizational Gameboard*. Englewood Cliffs, NJ, Educational Technology Publications, Inc.

Kress, G. (1982) *Learning to Write*. London, Routledge.

Kress, G. (1987) 'Genre in a social theory of language: a reply to John Dixon'. In I. Reid (ed.) *The Place of Genre in Learning: Current Debates*. Victoria: Deakin University.

Kress, G. (1989) 'Texture and meaning'. In R. Andrews (ed.) *Narrative and Argument*. Milton Keynes, Open University Press.

Kress, G. (1991) 'Two kinds of power'. *The English Magazine*, 24, 4–7.

Lakoff, G. and Johnson, M. (1980) *Metaphors We Live By*. Chicago, University of Chicago Press.

Larkin, P. (1964) *The Whitsun Weddings*. London, Faber.

Littlefair, A.B. (1991) *Reading All Types of Writing*. Milton Keynes, Open University Press.

Lodge, D. (1988) *Nice Work*. London, Secker and Warburg.

Longacre, R.E. (1983) *The Grammar of Discourse*. London, Pergamon Press.

Lunzer, E. and Gardner, K. (1979) *The Effective Use of Reading*. London, Heinemann Educational.

Macken, M. *et al.* (1990) *A Genre-based Approach to Teaching Writing in Years 3–6: Books 1 & 2*. NSW Department of Education.

Mackey, W.F. (1967) *Bilingualism as a World Problem/Le Bilinguisme: Phenomene Mondiale*. Montreal, Harvest House.

March, J.G. and Simon, H.A. (1958) *Organizations*. New York, Wiley.

Mares, P. (1988) 'Literary literature and first year studies'. *Typereader: Journal of the Centre for Studies in Literary Education*, 1, 19–33.

Marland, M. (1991) 'Helping a hand to literacy'. *Education Guardian*, 22 January.

Martin, J.R. (1985/9) *Factual Writing: Exploring and Challenging Social Reality*. Australia, Oxford University Press.

Martin, J. (1990) 'Literacy in science'. In F. Christie (ed.) *Literacy in a Changing World*. Slough, National Foundation for Educational Research.

Martin, J.R., Christie, F. and Rothery, J. (1987) 'Social processes in education'. In I. Reid (ed.) *The Place of Genre in Learning: Current Debates*. Victoria, Deakin University.

McClelland, J.L. (1987) 'The case for interactionism in language processing'. In M. Coultard (ed.) *The Psychology of Reading*. London, Lawrence Erlbaum Associates.

McLeay, A. (1986) *Gary Greenfingers says: Let's Grow*. Leeds, Arnold-Wheaton.

McLeay, A. (1987) *Festivals*. Leeds, Arnold-Wheaton.

Medway, P. (1991) 'Modes of engagement through language'. *Educational Review*, 43(2), 159–69.

Meek, M. (1988) *How Texts Teach What Readers Learn*. Stroud, Thimble Press.

Moffett, J. (1968) *Teaching the Universe of Discourse*. Boston, Houghton Mifflin.

Moi, T. (1985) *Sexual/textual Politics: Feminist Literary Theory*. London, Methuen.

Monash University (1988) *Sound*. University of Monash Broadsheet 20.

Montgomery, C.A., Wernerfelt, B. and Balakrishnan, S. (1989) 'Strategy content and the research process: a critique and commentary'. *Strategic Management Journal*, 10, 189–97.

Moorfield, J. (1987). 'Implications for schools of research findings in bilingual education'. In W. Hirst (ed.) *Living Languages: Bilingualism and Community Languages in New Zealand*. Auckland, Heinemann.

National Education Crisis Committee (1986) *People's English for People's Power: Draft Proposals*. Press Release, 27 November.

Neate, B. (1990) 'The diversity of registers found in primary children's information books'. *Reading*, 24, 3.

Neville, M. (1988) *Assessing and Teaching Language, Literacy and Oracy in Schools*. Basingstoke, Macmillan Educational.

Newman, J.H. (1873) *The Idea of a University Defined and Illustrated* (3rd edn). London, Pickering.

Newman, J.H. (1915) *On the Scope and Nature of University Education*. London, J.M. Dent & Sons Ltd.

NFER (1991) *An Inquiry into LEA evidence on Standards of Reading of Seven Year Old Children*. Berkshire, NFER Nelson.

Nutt, P.C. (1989) 'Selecting tactics to implement strategic plans'. *Strategic Management Journal*, 10, 145–61.

Nuttall, D.L. (1989) 'The validity of assessments'. In P. Murphy and B. Moon (eds) *Developments in Learning and Assessment*. London, Hodder and Stoughton.

Ontario Ministry of Education (1977) *Curriculum Guideline for the Senior Division, English*. Toronto, Government of Ontario.

Ontario Ministry of Education (1987) *Curriculum Guideline, English, Intermediate and Senior Divisions, Grades 7–12*. Toronto, Government of Ontario.

Ontario Provincial Advisory Committee on Race Relations (1987) *The Development of a Policy on Race and Ethnocultural Equity: Report of the Provincial Advisory Committee on Race Relations*. Toronto, Government of Ontario.

Pecheux, M. (1975) *Language Semantics and Ideology: Stating the Obvious*, translated by H. Nagpal (1982). London, Macmillan.

Perera, K. (1980) 'The assessment of linguistic difficulty in reading material'. *Educational Review*, 32(2).

Pocock, J.G.A. (1984) 'Verbalizing a political act: towards a politics of speech'. In M.J. Shapiro (ed.) *Language and Politics*. Oxford: Basil Blackwell.

Pumfrey, P.D. (1990) 'Literacy and the National Curriculum: the challenge of the 1990s'. In P.D. Pumfrey and C.D. Elliott (eds) *Children's Difficulties in Reading, Spelling and Writing*. Lewes, Falmer Press.

Quinn, J.B. (1980) *Strategics for Change: Logical Incrementalism*. Homewood, IL, Irwin.

Reid, I. (ed.) (1987) *The Place of Genre in Learning: Current Debates*. Centre for Studies in Literary Education. Victoria, Deakin University.

Reilley, R.G. (1985) 'Control processing versus information processing models of reading'. *The Journal of Research in Reading*, 8(1), 3–19.

Ricks, C.E. and Michaels, L. (1990) *The State of the Language*. London, Faber.

Robinson, J.C. (1987) *Radical Literary Education: A Classroom Experiment with Wordsworth's Ode*. Madison, WI, University of Wisconsin Press.

Romaine, S. (1989) *Bilingualism*. Oxford, Blackwell.

Rosenblatt, L.M. (1978) *The Reader, the Text, the Poem: The Transactional Theory of the Literary Work*. Carbondale, IL, Southern Illinois University Press.

Rosenblatt, L.M. (1985) *Literature as Exploration* 3rd edn. New York, Modern Language Association.

Sanford, A.J. and Garrod, S.C. (1981) *Understanding Written Language*. Chichester, John Wiley and Sons.

Saunders, G. (1982) *Bilingual Children: Guidance for the Family*. Clevedon, Avon, Multilingual Matters.

Scahill, J.H. (1989) 'Educational policy studies. Review of Giroux, H.A. (1988). "Teachers as intellectuals: Toward a critical pedagogy of learning"'. *Educational Studies*, 20(1), 91–7.

Schleiermacher, F.D.E. (1809/1977) *Hermeneutics: The Handwritten Manuscripts*, translated by J. Duke and J. Fortiman. The American Academy of Religion, Issoula, Montana, Scholars Press.

Scholes, R. (1985) *Textual Power: Literary Theory and the Teaching of English*. New Haven, Yale University Press.

Schön, D. (1983) *The Reflective Practitioner: How Professionals Think in Action*. New York, Basic Books.

Shuy, R.W. (1987) 'Conversational power in FBI covert tape recordings'. In L. Kedar (ed.) *Power Through Discourse*. Norwood NJ, Ablex.

Singh, G. (1988) *Language, Race and Education*. Birmingham, Jaysons.

Sondergaard, B. (1981) 'Decline and fall of an individual bilingualism'. *Journal of Multilingual and Multicultural Development*, 2, 297–302.

Strube, P. (1990) 'Narrative in science education'. *English in Education*, 24(1), 53–66.

Tannen, D. (1987) 'Remarks on discourse and power'. In Kedar, L. (ed.) *Power Through Discourse*. Norwood, NJ, Ablex.

Tannen, D. (1990) *You Just Don't Understand. Women and Men in Conversation*. New York, William Morrow Inc.

The Globe and Mail (1988) 'Schoolboard rejects bid to ban novel', 1 July.

Thompson, J.B. (1984) *Studies in the Theory of Ideology*. Cambridge, Polity Press.

Thomson, J. (1987) *Understanding Teenagers' Reading Processes and the Teaching of Literature*. Australia, Methuen.

Tolley, G. (1989) 'Learning and assessment'. In *Developments in Learning and Testing*. London, Hodder and Stoughton.

Tolstoy, L. (1862/1967) *Tolstoy on Education*, translated by L. Wiener. Chicago, The University of Chicago Press.

Tompkins, J.P. (1980) *Reader-response Criticism: From Formalism to Post-structuralism*. Baltimore, Johns Hopkins University Press.

Unsworth, L. (1990) 'Learning the culture through literacy development: Information books for beginning readers', paper presented to the thirteenth World Congress of the International Reading Association, Stockholm, 3–6 July.

Varenne, H. (1987) 'Analytic ambiguities in the communication of familial power'. In L. Kedar (ed.) *Power Through Discourse*. Norwood, NJ, Ablex.

Ventola, E. (1987) *The Structure of Social Interaction. A Systemic Approach to the Semiotics of Service Encounters*. London, Pinter.

Verwoerd, H. (1954) Speech delivered to the Senate, 7 June. In B. Rose and R. Tunmer (eds) (1975) *Documents in South African Education*. Johannesburg, A.D. Donker.

Volosinov, L. (1973) *Marxism and the Philosophy of Language*, translated by L. Matejka and I.R. Titunik (1986). Cambridge, MA, Harvard University Press.

Vygotsky, L.S. (1965) *Thought and Language*, translated by Hanfman and Vaker. Cambridge, Mass., Massachusetts Institute of Technology.

Weedon, C. (1987) *Feminist Practice and Post-structuralist Theory*. Oxford, Blackwell.

Wells, G. (1987) *The Meaning Makers*. London, Hodder and Stoughton.

Whitelaw, W. (1989) *The Whitelaw Memoirs*. London, Aurum Press.

Widdowson, P. (ed.) (1982) *Re-reading English*. New York, Methuen.

Wilkinson, A. (1986) *The Writing of Writing*. Milton Keynes, Open University Press.

Zuboff, S. (1988) *In the Age of the Smart Machine: the Future of Work and Power*. New York, Basic Books.

Index

social empowerment, 86
social order, 53
social processes, genres as, 73
social relevance, 63, 64, 68
social values, 11–24
sociolinguistic study (multilingualism
   and bilingualism study), 39–40
Sondergaard, B., 37
South Africa (people's English), 50–9
South African Democratic Teachers'
   Union (SADTU), 51
Soweto Day (16 June), 56
Soweto uprising (1976), 51
speech, 37, 92
   direct, 14–15, 16, 75, 77–8, 81
   talking for social action, 25–35
Spender, Stephen, 5–6
staff development strategies, 21
staged structures, 87, 88, 91, 92–3
Standard English, 4, 5–6, 8, 9–10, 41,
   43, 45, 46, 49
Statements of Attainment, 100–1
Stibbs, A., 25
stories (learning to read), 72, 74, 75, 76
story genres, 81, 90
strategic discourse, 23
strategic management, 13, 22–4
Strategic Management Journal, 22
strategic planning, 13
Stratta, L., 94
Straw, S., 61
Strube, P., 77
subject (generic traits), 105, 106
subject position, 54–7
Swain, M., 37
Swann Report (1985), 41, 43
sympathetic identification, 64, 68
'systematic thought', 75
systemic level (organizational change),
   18–20
systemic linguistic theories, 86–7

talking for social action, 25–35
Tanner, D., 23, 57
teach-test-and-reteach cycle, 109
teacher tutoring, 111
teachers
   assessment by, 96, 101–5, 106

multi/bilingualism study, 43–6
 – reader, 88
 Section II, 41, 43, 44
 use of genre, 101–51
Technical and Vocational Initiative, 27
   DEFT Report, 25, 28–35
'temporal conjunctive relations', 91
temporal organizations, 105, 106
tertiary institutions (Australia), 19, 21
test-retest situation, 96
text
   engagement with, 61, 62, 64, 66
   ephemeral, 30–1
   narrative, *see* narrative texts
   non-chronological, 75, 78, 79
   non-fiction, 71–83
   non-narrative, 71, 101–3
Thompson, J.B., 53, 54
Thomson, J., 68
through-put rates, 14
time on task, 109
Tolley, George, 96
Tolstoy, L., 95
Tompkins, J.P., 61
topical organizations, 105, 106
totalizing discourse, 6–8
transaction/transactional model, 26–7,
   60
transformation (literature education),
   61–3, 64, 65, 66, 67, 68
'transition' policy, 42

understanding (assessment of), 98–9
unemployment, 11
Unified National System (of higher
   education), 18, 20
Unsworth, L., 76–7
'up' expression, 54–5, 56

valley dwellers (in circular structures),
   23–4
values and goals (organizational
   structures), 13
van Riebeeck Day, 56
Varenne, H., 21
Ventola, E., 73
verbalizations, 14
Verwoerd, H., 54